-0. NOV. 1982 Home Office

Scottish Home and Health Department

Nuclear Weapons

London: Her Majesty's Stationery Office

© *Crown Copyright 1974*
First published 1956
Third Edition 1974
Fourth Impression 1980

ISBN 0 11 340557 X

Preface

1. Information obtained from the study of the results of British and American trials of nuclear weapons of different types and power has rendered obsolete some of the information in the Manual of Civil Defence Vol I Pamphlet No I "Nuclear Weapons". This booklet reviews the effects of nuclear detonations in the light of this information and also presents the latest considerations on the control of radiological exposure. Chapter 10 on 'Hazards to Food, Water, Crops and Livestock' similarly incorporates current knowledge. The booklet is intended primarily for use by persons who are involved in home defence planning, but it may be of interest to others.

2. The booklet describes a wide range of nuclear weapon effects. In cross references in the text the first number denotes the chapter and the second the number of the paragraph in that chapter.

Contents

Tables

Figures

Plates

1 General Features of Nuclear Weapons

Introduction

1.1 Conventional high explosive (H.E.) weapons contain substances which, on detonation, release energy as a result of chemical changes. The atoms of carbon, hydrogen, oxygen and nitrogen in the original H.E. are released and recombine to form the waste products of the explosion.

1.2 Nuclear explosives, weight for weight, liberate vastly greater amounts of energy than conventional explosives and this energy comes from the inner core or nucleus of each atom. In nuclear explosions, measurable quantities of matter are converted into energy, but only a few of the known elements have atoms capable of releasing large quantities of nuclear energy.

1.3 Some knowledge of the structure of atoms helps towards an understanding of nuclear weapons and their effects; moreover, it is difficult to describe some aspects of these weapons without using scientific terms like isotopes, neutrons, and electrons. Appendix 1 contains brief notes on the structure of matter, fission reactions and critical sizes of fissile materials, and on thermonuclear fusion reactions.

Fission (or atomic) weapons

1.4 The large atoms of the heavy metals, plutonium (made artificially in a nuclear reactor) and uranium, can split into two not quite equal parts, a process which is called FISSION. This is the process which takes place in the explosion of atomic weapons.

Fusion (or hydrogen) weapons

1.5 Another process by which nuclear energy can be released is called FUSION, because certain kinds of hydrogen atoms (called deuterium and tritium) can fuse together at temperatures of millions of degrees. The temperatures attained in the detonation of atomic fission weapons are nearly as high as those at the centre of the sun. Fusion or hydrogen weapons therefore need a small atomic or fission charge as an initiator, and for this reason they are sometimes

1

known as fission-fusion devices and are termed THERMONUCLEAR weapons.

1.6 For equal weights of nuclear explosive charge, the fusion or H-bomb releases about two-and-a-half times as much energy as the fission or atomic bomb. Another important difference is that the size of a purely fission type bomb is limited because, above a certain critical size, a lump of fissile material is self-disruptive. A fusion or hydrogen bomb, on the other hand, has no such limit to its size other than that imposed by the method of delivery on to the target. It is possible also to have a fission-fusion-fission type of thermonuclear weapon in which a fusion or hydrogen bomb, containing a core of fissile Uranium-235 as an initiator, is encased in Uranium-238. This U-238 casing also undergoes fission from the high speed neutrons produced in the hydrogen fusion detonation and, since the casing might be many times heavier than the fissile core of U-235, correspondingly larger quantities of fission products would be released as fallout from such a weapon.

Energy distribution in a nuclear detonation

1.7 The large quantities of nuclear energy released in a detonation on or near ground level are distributed approximately in the following way:

  45 per cent in the form of blast and shock waves
  35 per cent as light and heat radiation
   5 per cent as initial nuclear radiations
  15 per cent as residual radiation from fission products

1.8 Blast and shock waves, and to a lesser extent light and heat flash, are effects common to both conventional H.E. and nuclear detonations, but only a nuclear detonation gives rise to nuclear radiation. Initial radiations include the instantaneous radiation, most of which is delivered within 10 seconds, and, by accepted definition, all other nuclear radiations emitted within a minute of the detonation. The residual radiation comes from radio-active fission products, which, together with the other contents of the bomb, are vaporised by the intense heat in the fireball; when they condense on debris or dust, these particles will fall to the ground as radioactive FALLOUT over an extensive area. The residual radiation decays rapidly at first, but more slowly with time, and it may continue to be a hazard for a long period.

Weapon power or yield

1.9 The power of a nuclear weapon is the total amount of energy released on detonation, including all the forms of energy mentioned

2

in paragraph 1.7. A weapon can be 'tailor-made' to cause the maximum damage to a particular type of target.

1.10 The more familiar units of energy (eg the kilowatt hour) are too small to express the vast quantities of energy released in the detonation of a nuclear bomb. Two units are commonly used; the kiloton (KT) unit equivalent to 1,000 tons of TNT, and the megaton (MT) unit equivalent to the energy released by the detonation of 1,000,000 tons of TNT.

1.11 The bombs dropped on Hiroshima and Nagasaki had a power of about 20 KT. Since then there have been trials with thermonuclear weapons of up to about 65 MT in power, but there are relatively few targets in the world which would appear to justify the use of so powerful a weapon.

1.12 In this booklet the term 'kiloton' is reserved for those weapons below 500 KT in power and more powerful types are described in 'megatons'; a 500 KT weapon being classed as half-megaton ($\frac{1}{2}$ MT). In later chapters the distances from the detonation at which specific effects are likely to be produced have been tabulated for weapons of the following powers:

20 KT, 100 KT, $\frac{1}{2}$ MT, 1 MT, 2 MT, 5 MT, 10 MT and 20 MT

The fireball and the cloud

1.13 The contents of a nuclear weapon are vaporised in the luminous fireball which rapidly expands and cools to form the familiar radioactive mushroom cloud and stem. The fireball on expansion becomes lighter than the surrounding atmosphere and starts to shoot upwards at speeds which may reach 300 miles per hour. Its maximum size, its duration as a luminous fireball, the speed at which it will rise and the height to which the cloud will ascend, depend upon the power of the weapon and, to some extent, upon the height of burst and prevailing meteorological conditions (Plate 1).

1.14 The temperature of the air in northern temperate latitudes falls gradually with increasing altitude and, at a height of about 35,000 to 40,000 ft, there is a region called the tropopause where it remains constant at about −60°C: above this is the stratosphere. The cloud produced by the detonation of a KT weapon, if it does reach the tropopause, will not penetrate far but will flatten out into the well-known mushroom shape. The clouds from MT weapons, on the other hand, may penetrate the tropopause and rise to heights of 20 miles or more, into the stratosphere, depending upon the power of the weapon.

Types and heights of burst

1.15 The effects produced by the detonation of a nuclear weapon can vary considerably according to the height at which it is burst. Nuclear weapons may be fused to burst:

a.   on or near the ground;

b.   in shallow water in a harbour, lake or river, or in deep water at sea;

c.   high in the air;

d.   very high, on the fringe of the earth's atmosphere.

For each weapon of a specific power there is a maximum height of burst, about four-fifths of the fireball radius, above which the fireball will not suck up soil particles on which fission products can condense to form the large radioactive fallout particles, which account for close-in and significant fallout. These maximum heights are shown in Table 1 for a range of weapon powers.

Table 1

Power of bomb	Maximum height for contaminating burst (in feet)
20 KT	600
100 KT	1,100
½ MT	2,200
1 MT	2,900
2 MT	3,800
5 MT	5,400
10 MT	7,200
20 MT	9,300

Ground bursts

1.16 A ground burst is one in which the weapon is detonated either on the ground or at such a low altitude that an appreciable part of the fireball touches the surface beneath it. As the fireball shoots upward it not only carries up with it much vaporised soil material, it also leaves behind a partial vacuum, and this causes a strong wind directed inwards and upwards towards the centre of the fireball. As this wind speed may be 200 or more miles per hour, it will carry with it large quantities of dust and debris on which the radioactive fission products can also condense; these radioactive particles will be ultimately deposited on the ground as fallout.

1.17 Large pieces of debris and particles measuring over 2 millimetres will probably fall in the vicinity of the crater: smaller particles, carried to various altitudes in the cloud, will fall at lesser speeds depending upon their size and shape. In falling they will be carried along by the prevailing winds, which may differ considerably both in strength and direction at different heights.

1.18 In a ground burst, an appreciable amount of the total energy released is dissipated in forming a crater and some of the initial heat and nuclear radiations will be absorbed by the material displaced and lifted from the crater. Consequently, the ranges of blast damage, fires and skin burns and the effects from initial nuclear radiation will be less than they would be for an air burst of the same power.

Water bursts

1.19 Detonations in shallow water or at such a height that the fireball touches the water surface are termed 'water bursts'. Large quantities of water and, in shallow water, bottom mud will be carried up into the fireball. When the vaporised water in the cloud reaches a high altitude it will condense to rain and bring down with it radioactive fission products, some of which may be gelatinous or dissolved in the rain drops. The fallout pattern on neighbouring land will be less extensive in area but more intensely radioactive than from a ground burst. Wet fallout may be also more difficult to remove, especially from rough or retentive surfaces, than the relatively dry particles which occur in fallout from a ground burst.

1.20 A nuclear weapon may burst in deep water and, apart from the absence of mud, the effects will be similar to those from a surface burst except that a larger amount of the total energy released will be expended in vaporising water, in producing a shock wave through the water and in forming surface waves. Most of the fission products will be trapped in the water near the burst and will diffuse and disperse rapidly.

Air bursts

1.21 An air burst is one in which the weapon is detonated so that the fireball is well clear of the surface beneath it. There will be very few dust particles to which the vaporised fission products can adhere and they will therefore condense to minute particles with such a low speed of fall that they will been dispersed far and wide by the winds before they reach the ground. No significant fallout hazard will occur from this type of burst except perhaps to the extent that heavy rainfall may carry down some of the fission products from the lower parts of the cloud before it disperses.

1.22 The height and the power of an air burst determine the extent of blast damage at the surface and this in turn depends upon the type of terrain. For a 20 KT weapon the optimum height to produce the heaviest blast damage in residential areas in the United Kingdom is about 1,000 ft: this may be compared with 600 ft, the maximum height for a contaminating burst (see paragraph 1.15 and Table 1). The corresponding figures for a 10 MT weapon are 1.5 miles and 1.36 miles: even these small differences between the optimum heights for damage and contamination become insignificant for weapons of 20 MT and above.

'Clean' and 'dirty' bombs

1.23 Fission products are released by all existing types of nuclear weapon. 'Dirty' bombs (see Appendix 1 paragraph 14) produce the larger amounts of radioactive fallout and so-called 'clean' bombs produce little, but the latter emit greater amounts of neutrons which induce radioactivity in soil. Any dividing line between 'clean' and 'dirty' bombs is therefore arbitrary, but fission-fusion-fission weapons mentioned in paragraph 1.6 are 'dirty' by any standards.

Possible methods of attack with nuclear weapons

1.24 Weapon design has improved so much that it is possible to incorporate megaton warheads in a variety of weapons, including ballistic missiles with a range of several thousand miles. Possible means of delivery are listed below:

i.   manned bombers which may be supersonic;

ii. pilotless aircraft released from land or from ships—SSMs (Surface to Surface Missiles);

iii. guided bombs released from aircraft several hundred miles from the target—ASMs (Air to Surface Missiles);

iv. ballistic missiles—IRBMs (Intermediate Range Ballistic Missiles) and ICBMs (Inter-Continental Ballistic Missiles) released from land, ships off-shore, submerged submarines or satellites; and

v.   saboteurs.

1.25 Winged missiles can be guided to the target. However, since they depend on air to feed the engine, to support the wing loading and to exert forces on control surfaces, they are limited in speed and height of operation and are therefore more vulnerable to counter attack than ballistic missiles. The latter can be guided into the correct direction and attitude to reach the target as long as the rocket motor is operating; thereafter they must follow a ballistic path like a shell from a gun. However, since ballistic missiles travel for most of their range at altitudes of several hundred miles where there is practically no air resistance and can reach maximum speeds of 15,000 miles per hour, they reach their targets in a matter of minutes.

1.26 To counter attacks from IRBMs and ICBMs within the time available between launching and impact, it is necessary to detect the weapon, to compute its ballistic path and to fire and detonate as far away as possible from the target a defensive missile which is close enough to its path to destroy it.

Factors affecting the results of a nuclear attack

1.27 The damage to life and property that might be caused by nuclear detonations would depend upon:

i. the number and power of the bombs;

ii. the type of burst (air, water or ground) of each bomb and its location;

iii. the prevailing weather conditions, particularly wind strengths and directions at levels through which radioactive particles might fall;

iv. the method of attack and the actual public warning of attack, which might be very short; and

v. the measures for self-protection taken before and maintained after the attack.

Estimation of ranges of effects of bombs of different powers

1.28 After an attack with nuclear weapons, for each detonation information would be needed on:

a. the power or yield of the weapon;

b. the location of burst (ground zero—GZ);

c. the time of burst;

d. the height of burst;

e. the wind strengths and directions at all levels up to the top of the highest radioactive cloud.

How this information would be obtained is described briefly in Chapter 3.

1.29 When this information is available, estimates can be made of the extent of varying degrees of structural damage, of road blockage, of fires and skin burns as well as the ranges of lethal and sickness effects from initial radiation. Subsequently estimates of the extent of the residual radiation hazard can be made from the forecasted fallout pattern.

1.30 Tables showing the approximate ranges of the major effects of 20 KT, 100 KT, ½ MT, 1 MT, 2 MT, 5 MT, 10 MT and 20 MT weapons are included in later chapters for ready reference. For weapons of intermediate powers, the ranges can either be estimated roughly by interpolation, or they can be calculated from the simple principles and scaling laws from which the tables were derived (see Appendix II).

The 'Inverse Square' Law

1.31 The intensity of radiation received by a man exposed to a single source such as the fireball of a nuclear weapon decreases rapidly the further away he is from that source. If the distance is doubled the intensity falls to a quarter of its previous strength and if the distance is trebled it falls to a ninth ($\frac{1}{3} \times \frac{1}{3}$). In other words, it decreases by a factor which is proportional to the square of the distance from the source. This 'inverse square' law applies to all forms of radiation, light, heat, initial and residual nuclear radiations; each radioactive fallout particle can be regarded as a source. This is one of the reasons why it is desirable to shelter in the basement or in an inner room of a house to get as far away as possible from sources of penetrating gamma radiation such as fallout on the roof and around the outside walls.

1.32 In practice, other factors make the dose of thermal or nuclear radiation received by a man decrease more rapidly than would be predicted from the 'inverse square' law. The air itself attenuates radiation. For example, neutrons are absorbed by the atoms of nitrogen, gamma rays are scattered by the atoms of oxygen and nitrogen in the air, and heat radiation may be scattered or reflected back by dust particles and moisture droplets in the air. The extent of fires and the degree of burns depend not only on the total amount of heat received but also on the rate at which it falls on a surface. These additional influences are discussed in Chapters 4 and 5.

Scaling laws for the effects of different bomb powers

1.33 Scaling laws have been devised for estimating the ranges at which specific effects will result from nuclear weapons of different powers. They are based on scientific principles modified by the results of field trials. The range tables in later chapters have been calculated using these scaling laws and based on the observed effects of 1 KT and 1 MT nuclear detonations.

1.34 Scaling laws for the more important effects of nuclear detonations are given in Appendix II but, since most of these effects are proportional to the cube root of the weapon power, this 'cube root' law is outlined below.

The 'cube root' law (of weapon power)

1.35 The power of a nuclear weapon is defined as the total energy released in detonation. Thus, a 10 MT bomb is 500 times as powerful as a 20 KT bomb and so liberates 500 times as much energy in each of the forms of radiation, blast and fission products. Now the cube root of 500 ($\sqrt[3]{500}$) is nearly 8 and it has been found that the two weapons produce the same peak pressure (blast intensity) at distances from ground zero which differ by a factor of 8. In other words, the peak pressure at, say, 1 mile from the 20 KT detonation will be the same as the peak pressure, at $1 \times \sqrt[3]{500}$ or 8 miles from the 10 MT detonation. Similarly a 1 MT weapon, which is 1,000 times as powerful as a 1 KT weapon will give the same peak pressure at a distance from GZ which is $\sqrt[3]{1,000}$ or 10 times greater. Stating this as a formula, a detonation X times as powerful as another will create the same peak pressure as the latter at $\sqrt[3]{X}$ times the distance from ground zero.

1.36 The structural damage caused at any point by a nuclear detonation is determined largely by the maximum shock pressure at the point in question, but the duration of the shock wave is also significant in the case of larger buildings. Both the duration of the shock wave and the time which it takes to arrive are increased by a factor of $\sqrt[3]{X}$, for a weapon X times as powerful as another weapon at points where the peak pressure from each of these weapons happens to be the same.

1.37 Areas enclosing the same degree of building damage also have radii from GZ which vary according to the 'cube root' law of weapon yield and, hence, the extent of such areas can be calculated for weapons of different powers.

1.38 The diameter of the crater caused by a ground burst can also be determined by the 'cube root' law. Separate and more complicated scaling laws are necessary for estimating the depth of the crater, the maximum size of the fireball, the dimensions of the radioactive cloud after it has stopped ascending and the effects of different wind speeds on the shape of the fallout pattern. These are given in Appendix II, and, where possible, they have been incorporated in the range tables in the later chapters.

2 Biological Effects of Nuclear Radiations

Introduction

2.1 The human body is a highly complex organisation of cells and of delicate controlling mechanisms which are based on physical and chemical processes. The primary biological effect of nuclear radiations is to release within the cells of the body electrical charges, which interfere with the vital functions of the cells and cause many secondary functional disorders, as well as reducing resistance to infection and disease. Hence, the correlation of cause and effect is difficult and sometimes impossible.

Units: roentgens and curies

2.2 The curie is a measure of the quantity of radioactive matter present, the roentgen (r) is a unit of radiation exposure dose. The intensity of radiation, or dose-rate at any moment, is measured in roentgens per hour (rph). Another unit of dose called the rad is in use, but for home defence purposes the rad and the roentgen can be regarded as the same. Throughout this handbook only the symbols 'r' for doses and 'rph' for dose-rates will be used.

2.3 The quantity of radioactivity released in a nuclear fission detonation is about 300 megacuries, ie 300,000,000 curies, for each kiloton of bomb power.

Relation between dose-rate and deposited activity

2.4 When radioactive fallout is deposited uniformly over a large flat smooth area, the dose-rate at 3 ft above the surface will be about 10 rph for every curie of activity per square yard of surface. On uneven, ploughed or rough ground, bumps and ridges will absorb some of the slant rays and this relationship between dose-rate and deposit is reduced to about 6 rph per curie per square yard.

Individual sensitivity: sub-lethal doses

2.5 Living creatures differ in their sensitivity to radiation. Therefore it is necessary to employ a statistical method of measuring its biological effects. Similar methods are used in public health and

10

insurance and in determining the effective or lethal dose (LD) of poisons and of chemical or biological warfare agents. For example, a few are sensitive to relatively small doses of radiation or poisons while, at the other extreme, a few are capable of surviving heavy doses which would kill most of their kind. It is difficult, therefore, to specify within the range of possible lethal doses whether any particular individual in a group would die, but the dose which would be lethal for 50 per cent of the group can be estimated within approximate limits; this is called the LD 50 or the dose at which each individual has a fifty-fifty chance of survival. Higher doses can be tolerated if a part of the body, in particular the abdomen, is well shielded. Radiation on the whole body is more serious than radiation limited to, say, one side.

2.6 The best estimate that can be given at present for this lethal dose of whole body radiation for human beings is that the LD 50 lies somewhere between 350r and 550r if the dose is received quickly, within the space of an hour or two. The LD 50 becomes progressively larger as the radiation is spread at correspondingly lower dose-rates over weeks or months. The reason for this increase in tolerance is that the body is able, in time, to recover, at least partially, from most types of injury including those caused by radiation.

2.7 There is general concern among medical experts that significant increases in radiation dosage would cause grave genetic damage. However, it is not yet possible to define this hazard in quantitative terms. The normal hazards of working in nuclear power stations and in the use of radioactive isotopes in medicine and industry have little bearing on the dose-rate criteria which would have to apply to the nation in a nuclear war. In order to lessen the risks, the population should seek the best possible cover during the period of high dose-rates after attack and should follow a regime of limited daily outdoor exposure for some time thereafter. Inevitably any assessment of the tolerance dose limit for essential outdoor workers under fallout conditions should balance the short term advantages of carrying out immediate operational tasks against the longer term radiation damage which they might sustain. Obviously exposure should be avoided if at all possible and everywhere kept at a minimum.

Relation between dose and effects
2.8 In recent years research has been undertaken into the effect of radiation on a wide range of animals and into the results of accidents to human beings. These investigations led to the conclusion that the body exhibits a two-stage response to radiation:

a. the *first* stage is a relatively quick response to radiation doses received within about one day, that awakens a dormant tolerance to an initial exposure, making the body insensitive to the first dose up to about 150r. This first stage response is virtually the same in all species.

b. the *second* stage is a slow response, consisting of the gradual replacement of cells killed by previous radiation, by virtue of the division and growth of neighbouring cells. This slow, dead-cell replacement phase represents recovery from injury in the normal sense, but the rate varies in different species. It is estimated that the recovery rate in human beings is at least equivalent to 10r per day.

Wartime emergency doses

2.9 As a result of these investigations, the following rules now apply for essential operational tasks during and immediately after a nuclear attack, as well as for assessing, at later stages, the relative radiological states and degree of radiation injury of different groups of people sheltering in heavy fallout areas. As a general rule a War Emergency Dose (WED) of 75r will be the maximum permissible in the execution of essential operational tasks, except in the circumstances outlined in i and ii below:

i. persons engaged on vital tasks may undertake a second period of duty, which could involve an additional WED of 75r, making a maximum total dose of 150r, provided there is a rest period of about 8 hours between the two periods of duty;

ii. persons, who have remained in shelter for several days and who have accumulated radiation doses while in shelter, may undertake essential tasks, provided that the total dose acquired *in shelter* and in performing the task does not exceed 150r, on the condition that this maximum dose of 150r is acquired over a period not exceeding 7 days;

iii. for assessing the relative radiological states of different groups of people at some number of days after a nuclear attack, the following formula may be used during the first 100 days post-attack:

OPERATIONAL EVALUATION DOSE (OED)$=(x-150-10t)$

where x represents the total accumulated dose expressed in r units, and the time after attack t is expressed in days for values up to 100.

2.10 When the OED calculated as above has a negative or zero value, there will be no apparent radiation injury and no physical or mental deterioration of the individual. Long term effects are not taken into account. When the calculated OED is positive, the value is a measure of the relative degree of injury; for example, some people may become ill while living in shelter but may recover in a week or two without medical or even nursing care, provided they have adequate drinking water and some food. Even at higher OED levels some people may recover if they are given skilled nursing and medical care. Many others will die.

Symptoms of radiation injury

2.11 The biological effects of nuclear radiation on the whole body may become apparent in four successive phases; malaise, delayed effects, long-term injury and genetic damage.

Radiation malaise

2.12 Radiation malaise, usually the first symptom, is caused by damage to the gastro-intestinal tract and may develop from a few hours to a day after exposure, depending upon the dose received. It may last two to three days and be followed by a period of well-being and apparent recovery. On average, radiation malaise will result from accumulated doses exceeding 150r. Its symptoms are fatigue, nausea, indigestion, loss of appetite and, as the dose increases, there may also be vomiting, diarrhoea and the discharge of blood. The times at which these symptoms occurred might be the only clue to the dose that a person had received.

Delayed illness effects

2.13 Delayed illness effects are caused mainly by injury to the body's blood-forming system. Heavy doses may cause serious illness after a latent period of several days. Lighter doses may cause milder illness up to four weeks after exposure. There may be a loss of body hair and blood spots, due to haemorrhages under the skin, may appear. While one cannot be precise, these symptoms may be expected to appear in some individuals exposed to acute doses in excess of 150r. The effects of doses in the region of 150r are not necessarily incapacitating. One of the problems in heavy fallout areas may be that doses, which are sufficient in themselves to cause serious illness, will also cause deterioration in the body's natural immunisation against certain diseases. With this deterioration, intestinal and respiratory infections could spread rapidly in crowded living conditions.

Long-term injuries to the individual

2.14 Long-term injuries include anaemia, leukaemia (a form of blood cancer developing three to six years after exposure) as well as tumours and cancers of the bones or tissues which may develop much later. It is estimated that for every one million people exposed to a dose of 100r, deaths from the long-term effects would occur as follows:

Leukaemia	2,000 deaths within 20 years
General Cancer	2,000 to 5,000 deaths to beyond 20 years
Thyroid Cancer	2,000 to 10,000 cases beyond 10 years
(*mainly in young children*)	depending upon the availability of special treatment.

For exposures in excess of 100r, these rates would probably be increased at least proportionately. Premature ageing and loss of vigour might be expected as effects of doses of around 400r, but whether as the direct effect of radiation or merely as a consequence of secondary effects and the reduced resistance to disease is not yet clear. Whether or not there is a threshold dose of radiation, which must be exceeded before these long-term effects will occur, is still an open question. In the light of present knowledge, it may be assumed for home defence planning purposes, that the increased risk of leukaemia and cancer should be discounted in the early years of post-strike recovery period in relation to the magnitude of casualties from the other effects of nuclear war.

Genetic damage

2.15 Genetic damage is caused by the effects of radiation on the body's germ cells, which transmit heritable characteristics to subsequent generations. It appears that the overall genetic damage caused by radiation at lower levels is directly proportional to the total population dose irrespective of whether this is received in larger doses by a few individuals or in smaller doses by a larger number of individuals. It has been estimated that the gene mutation rate would be doubled by a dose between 30r and 80r, and that for every million births there could be an additional 2,000 visibly defective children for each 100r to which the parents were exposed. This number would decrease slightly in each successive generation.

2.16 Until more is known about human genetics, avoidable exposure to radiation in war should obviously be restricted to the minimum number of people and preferably to those over 35 years of age. In performing essential operational tasks in war under fallout conditions, even in accordance with the conditions laid down in paragraph 2.9 above, these criteria should be remembered.

14

Radioactive strontium and iodine

2.17 In order to dispose of some of the myths surrounding radiation hazards, mention is made here of Strontium 90 and related isotopes. The radioactive strontium isotopes found among the fission products of a nuclear detonation are Strontium 89 which has a half-life (see paragraph 3.3) of about 51 days and Strontium 90 which has a half-life of about 28 years. Both of these emit beta particles (see paragraph 6, Appendix I) but no gamma radiation; some Sr90 may accumulate and persist in growing bone for many years, but the beta particles have a very short range and only affect the bone marrow, without reaching the germ cells. Radioactive strontium is therefore not a genetic hazard; nor is radioactive iodine, which tends to accumulate in the thyroid gland in the neck. The predominant form of radioactive iodine has a relatively short half-life of about eight days and could be a hazard, primarily to infants and young children with small thyroid glands. Although the ingestion of these and other radionuclides administers to some organs or to the whole body an internal dose, medical opinion regards the risk from such a dose in the aftermath of a nuclear attack as negligible compared with that from external gamma radiation (see paragraphs 10.1 and 10.2).

3 Detection and Measurement of the Effects of Nuclear Explosions

Assembling and reporting information about nuclear explosions and fallout

3.1 The United Kingdom Warning and Monitoring Organisation is responsible for providing details of nuclear bursts and for predicting the path and intensity of fallout. The Organisation has a country-wide network of monitoring posts reporting to local group controls which in turn report to sector controls. The Royal Observer Corps comprises the field reporting element and the data which they supply is evaluated at group and sector controls by scientists, meteorologists and other members of the Home Departments' warning teams.

3.2 On the explosion of a nuclear weapon, information relating to the power, location and height of burst would be reported from monitoring posts to the group controls, where it would be processed. With the aid of meteorological reports of the mean wind speeds and directions at various heights up to 100,000 feet, a broad prediction would be made of which areas were likely to be covered by fallout; then warnings of the approaching threat would be issued to the public. When the radiac instruments at the monitoring posts begin to record the presence of fallout, the times of arrival and, at short intervals, the dose-rates would be reported to the group and sector controls, where the boundaries of the fallout and its advancing fronts would be plotted on maps. Previous predictions would be amended and further warnings would be issued to the public as necessary. Detailed information about the fallout situation would be passed to local and central government wartime headquarters so that they too would be in a position to predict the likelihood and possible limits of fallout. Since individual monitoring posts are several miles apart, the broad picture obtained from this network would be supplemented in greater detail from information gathered within the county.

Radioactive decay rates: half lives of radioactive isotopes

3.3 It is possible to measure the rate at which radioactive matter disintegrates and decays into stable non-radioactive forms. The process of decay cannot be influenced by heat, pressure or chemical reaction. A convenient way of expressing this rate of decay is by the term 'half-life' that is the time by which half of the radioactive atoms originally present in the matter will have decayed. This time is independent of the amount of matter involved. The 'half-life' is a constant for each isotope; it is characteristic of that isotope and therefore offers a convenient means of identifying it.

3.4 About 200 isotopes, or different radioactive species, of the atoms of about 35 elements are released in a nuclear fission detonation and their half-lives vary from a fraction of a second to thousands of years. The rate of decay of the mixed fission products is rapid at first but it slows down in time as the shorter-lived isotopes disappear. A formula has been found, for times between 1 hour after detonation up to about 100 days, to express the average decay rate of all the various released isotopes. The formula can be used for the purposes of exercises and studies to estimate the activity at any later time, provided its value has been measured at a known time. This formula is $R_t = R_1.t^{-1.2}$, where R_1 is the nominal dose-rate in rph at 1 hour after burst and R_t is the dose-rate at any later time t hours (see paragraph 8.15).

Radiac calculator and seven-tenths rule

3.5 The use of the mathematical formula in the previous paragraph for estimating fission product decay requires either logarithmic tables or special graphs. Alternatively the circular radiac calculators Nos 1 and 2 may be used. (The blue side of the No 1 calculator should be disregarded.) For most purposes the 'seven-tenths rule' enables one to make a quick approximate calculation of the radiation level at any time, from a single measurement at a known time (see also paragraph 8.14). This rule states that the intensity of radiation falls by a factor of 10 as the time lengthens by a factor of 7. Its application is illustrated in Table 2 starting at 100 rph, 1 hour after detonation.

Table 2

Time after burst	Time factor	Dose-rate rph	Dose-rate factor
1 hour	1	100	1
1¾ hours	7/4	50	½
7 hours	7	10	1/10
2 days (49 hours)	7×7	1	1/100
2 weeks	7×7×7	0.1	1/1,000
14 weeks	7×7×7×7	0.01	1/10,000

3.6 Various instruments have been developed for determining the position and power of a nuclear explosion (including the height of

17

3*

burst), for detecting radioactivity and for measuring radiation inten-sity. Most of these instruments are standard equipment in monitoring posts. Radiac instruments for measuring radiation are made available to local and certain other public authorities.

4 Effects of Initial Nuclear Radiations

Introduction

4.1 Nuclear radiations are continuously emitted for long periods after the moment of detonation of a nuclear weapon. They are emitted from the fireball, from the radioactive particles in the cloud as it is dispersed by the winds, and from the radioactive fallout material deposited on the ground. For definitive purposes, a division between initial (sometimes called flash) and residual radiation has been placed arbitrarily at one minute after detonation (see paragraph 1.8).

4.2 Neutrons (see Appendix I) and gamma rays are emitted instantaneously on detonation and they are followed by gamma radiation from the newly-formed and intensely radioactive fission products in the fireball. Most of the neutrons are captured by the material of the weapon itself but others escape.

Neutrons and induced activity

4.3 Since neutrons are fundamental particles carrying no electrical charge, they are not affected by the positive nuclear charges or the surrounding clouds of negative electrons in the matter through which they pass. They are deflected or stopped only by direct collision. They can therefore penetrate considerable distances through the atmosphere, but are stopped more rapidly than gamma rays. For some distance around the point of detonation the neutron dose may be higher than the gamma flash dose, but beyond that the gamma hazard predominates. Thus, it may happen that the neutron hazard in buildings is greater quite close to the detonation of small tactical weapons with light cases which permit a higher proportion of the neutrons to escape. Otherwise, buildings which give reasonable protection from gamma radiation also give good protection against neutrons.

4.4 Those neutrons, which escape from the detonation and are not captured immediately, are slowed down and then captured by the nuclei of neighbouring atoms, which themselves then become unstable and radioactive. This process is called 'induced' activity and it will occur in the material underneath a ground burst or low airburst and may be mixed with fission products in fallout. In general, induced activity in the soil decays more rapidly than the average for fission products and becomes insignificant within a few days.

4.5 Another form of induced activity, with immediate instead of prolonged effect, is the capture of neutrons by nitrogen atoms in the atmosphere. This new nucleus is intensely radioactive and very quickly emits an extremely penetrating gamma radiation which intensifies and extends the range of the initial gamma flash.

Initial gamma radiation

4.6 Gamma rays can penetrate directly a considerable thickness of matter but they are weakened in doing so. They can also be scattered back to earth from the atmosphere. Protection behind a heavy obstacle in the line of sight will not be so good as all-round cover under a thick shield.

4.7 The biological effects of gamma radiation are outlined in Chapter 2, but there are several major differences between the effects of initial and residual radiation. First, initial gamma rays are more penetrating because they carry more energy and, therefore, they require a thicker shield to give the same degree of protection. Secondly, while residual radiation from a fallout area shines on an exposed person from all directions, the gamma flash from one explosion comes mainly from one direction (apart from any scatter from the atmosphere) and one side of the body may shield the other. On balance, residual radiation may be more injurious than gamma flash at the same total dose. The LD 50 (or dose which would be lethal to 50 per cent of those exposed) might be significantly greater than 450r on exposure to flash radiation and significantly less than 450r in residual radiation (see also paragraphs 2.5 and 2.6).

Weapon power and range of effects

4.8 Table 3 shows the radial distance at which an LD 50 of 450r and a wartime emergency dose of 75r would be received by people exposed to initial radiation in the open. When distances are rounded off to the nearest quarter of a mile, there are no differences between the effects of ground and air bursts. In comparing the two rows of figures for each weapon power, it will be noticed that because of absorption and attentuation in the air, the dose decreases more rapidly with distance than would be predicted by the 'inverse square' law (paragraph 1.31). It will also be seen from a comparison of the ranges in Tables 3, 5 (paragraph 5.7), and 9 (paragraph 7.11), that for megaton bombs the hazards from blast and heat effects would extend far beyond the range of possible injury from initial nuclear radiations. At Hiroshima and Nagasaki, because the bombs were air burst, there was little fallout but the effects of initial radiation were felt (see also paragraph 4.3).

Table 3 Distances (in miles) of initial gamma effects on people exposed, in the open, to a ground or air burst nuclear weapon

Weapon power	20 KT	100 KT	½ MT	1 MT	2 MT	5 MT	10 MT	20 MT
50 per cent survival (450r)	¾	1	1¼	1½	1¾	2	2¼	2¼
No appreciable risk of sickness (75r)	1	1¼	1½	1¾	2	2¼	2½	2½

Shielding against initial gamma radiation: half value thickness of shielding materials

4.9 The initial gamma rays from a nuclear detonation are more energetic and penetrating than the residual radiation from fallout. Both initial and residual radiations are reduced in intensity by passage through shielding materials and to an extent which depends on the density of the material. The thickness of shield needed to reduce the dose-rate in a beam of gamma rays by one half is called the 'half value' thickness of that particular shielding material and this is irrespective of the magnitude of that dose-rate (see also paragraphs 9.3 and 9.10).

4.10 The approximate half-value thicknesses of the materials commonly used for shielding (steel, concrete, earth and water) against initial gamma radiation are shown in Table 4.

Table 4

Shielding material	Half-value thickness against initial gamma radiation (INCHES)
Steel	1.5
Concrete	6.0
Earth	7.5
Water	13.0

Personal protection from initial nuclear radiation

4.11 Contrary to some scientific fiction, no satisfactory therapy is at present available to those who are to be or have just been exposed to a lethal dose of radiation. Adequate shielding is the only protection against initial radiation. It will be remembered that radiation decreases with distance from the detonation (paragraph 4.8). Suitable clothing provides no protection against gamma radiation; it may however prevent radioactive dust from getting on to the skin or into the body.

5 Effects of Thermal Radiation

Introduction

5.1 Thermal radiation or heat flash consists of visible light rays, invisible ultra-violet rays of shorter wave length and invisible infra-red rays of longer wave length: these rays all travel with the speed of light. The ultra-violet rays, which would otherwise be particularly injurious, are soon absorbed in the atmosphere. In milder form these effects are like sunburn. Consequently at distances beyond which people are killed outright by blast, the effective thermal radiation consists almost entirely of intense visible light and infra-red rays. Paragraph 1.7 states that about 35 per cent of the total energy released in a nuclear detonation is emitted in the form of light and heat radiation, which can cause fires and skin burns at considerable distances.

5.2 The intensity of the direct heat radiation received at any place may be enhanced, in a way similar to that of visible light, by reflection and scatter from clouds or from fog and dust particles in the atmosphere, or it may be reduced by passing through thick fog or heavy atmospheric pollution.

5.3 The maximum size of the fireball and the time it persists depend upon the weapon power. Appendix II, paragraph 3 contains a formula, based on observations at weapon trials, for calculating the maximum size of the fireball for a weapon of any given power. The fireball from a 20 KT weapon lasts about $1\frac{1}{2}$ seconds; the fireball from a 10 MT detonation persists for at least 20 seconds, although most of the heat energy is emitted during the first half of this time.

5.4 Thermal radiation, like visible light, is reflected by light colours and absorbed by dark ones so that dark coloured objects of otherwise comparable inflammability are more likely to catch fire than white or light coloured ones.

5.5 It has been explained (paragraph 1.31 and 1.32) that, in a clear atmosphere, the amount of heat which would fall on a man exposed to radiation from a nuclear detonation would decrease rapidly in relation to his distance from the fireball: it would be decreased by a factor which is proportional to the square of that distance. For example, if the distance were trebled the radiation would be reduced to one-ninth. In practice, the atmosphere is rarely clear. It contains some mist, dust and industrial pollution; the actual conditions at the time and one's position, in relation to clouds of these substances in the air and to the fireball, would determine whether one would receive more or less radiation than would be calculated from the 'inverse square' law. When the sun is hidden, the daylight is scattered. Hence, there is no simple scaling law for determining the thermal effects produced by weapons of different powers (see also paragraph 5.10 and paragraph 3 of Appendix II).

Skin burns

5.6 Skin burns can be of varying degrees of severity ranging from a mere reddening of the surface, a more painful blistering, to a much more serious charring of the full thickness of the skin, even extending to underlying tissue. It is obvious, from our experience in sunbathing, that the duration may be as important as the total amount of heat, in causing skin burns or igniting inflammable material. Three factors determine the severity of burns: the total amount of heat, the body area on which it falls and the duration of its application.

5.7 Table 5 shows the ranges in miles at which people in the open would suffer varying degrees of skin burn from ground burst weapons of different power.

Table 5   Range of heat effects on people in the open in a clear atmosphere: Radii in miles for ground burst weapons

Weapon power	20 KT	100 KT	$\frac{1}{2}$ MT	1 MT	2 MT	5 MT	10 MT	20 MT
Charring of skin	1	2	4	5	$6\frac{3}{4}$	$9\frac{1}{4}$	12	16
Blistering of skin	$1\frac{1}{4}$	$2\frac{1}{2}$	$4\frac{3}{4}$	$6\frac{1}{4}$	$8\frac{1}{4}$	12	16	20
Reddening of skin	$1\frac{3}{4}$	$3\frac{1}{4}$	$6\frac{1}{2}$	$8\frac{1}{2}$	11	16	20	25

For an air burst, under exceptionally clear conditions, the distances could be about 50% greater.

The fire situation

5.8 Table 6 shows the ranges of the main fire zones from ground burst weapons of differing powers. Table 7 shows similar data for air bursts. It will be noted that the ranges from an air burst weapon are greater than those from a ground burst weapon. Within the lower range, fires would be extinguished by the general destruction of the houses and buildings: isolated fires could occur out to a range where the static over-pressure is one pound per square inch (1 psi) (see also paragraph 7.11).

Table 6 Main fire zone: Ground burst weapon. Range in miles

Visibility	Weapon power							
	20 KT	100 KT	½ MT	1 MT	2 MT	5 MT	10 MT	20 MT
2 miles	⅜–¾	¾–1½	1¼–2½	1½–3	2–4	2¾–5	3½–5½	4½–6½
8 miles	⅜–⅞	¾–1¾	1¼–3	1½–4	2–5	2¾–7	3½–9	4½–10
32 miles	⅜–1	¾–2	1¼–3½	1½–5	2–6½	2¾–9	3½–12	4½–15

Table 7 Main fire zone: Air burst weapon. Range in miles

Visibility	Weapon power							
	20 KT	100 KT	½ MT	1 MT	2 MT	5 MT	10 MT	20 MT
2 miles	½–1¼	⅞–2¼	1½–4	1¾–5	2¼–7	3¼–8½	4–10	6–12
8 miles	½–1⅜	⅞–2½	1½–5	1¾–6½	2¼–8	3¼–12	4–15	6–17
32 miles	½–1⅝	⅞–3	1½–6	1¾–8	2¼–11	3¼–15	4–20	6–25

Thermal effects of weapons of different powers

5.9 A 10 MT weapon radiates 500 times as much heat as one of 20 KT. According to the 'inverse square' law (paragraph 1.31) a 10 MT weapon should produce the same amount of heat as a 20 KT weapon at a distance 22 times as great. Because the heat from the larger bomb is spread over a much longer period, 20 seconds compared with a 1½ second flash from the 20 KT bomb, more of the heat is dissipated or conducted away from the surface. This is another reason why no simple scaling law can be given for the ranges of thermal effects from weapons of different powers.

Personal protection from thermal radiation

5.10 To obtain protection from thermal radiation, one has only to move out of the direct path of the rays from the fireball and any kind of shade will suffice. People caught in the open should take any available cover and should protect their eyes by not looking at the fireball. In this way serious burns may be avoided, particularly from the longer-lasting fireball. It is also desirable to take cover from any flying debris.

5.11 The importance of keeping as much of the skin covered as possible is illustrated by the fact that the risk of death from burns increases in proportion to the body area which has been burned. If this is below 20 per cent, the chance of recovery with medical attention is high; although less for old people. Even with 50 per cent of the body surface burned, there is a 50 per cent chance of recovery. Clothing offers considerable protection if it is thick or loose fitting, the lighter the colour the better. Outer garments of wool are better than those of cotton, as wool may melt whereas cotton tends to ignite.

Fire protection and precautions

5.12 Primary fires in buildings would result from heat flash through windows and other openings igniting the contents. To reduce the risk, inflammable items should be placed as far as possible out of the direct path of any heat rays that might enter through windows or other openings. If windows and skylights are whitewashed or painted this would keep out about 80 per cent of the heat radiation. Although windows might be broken by the blast wave, this may not increase the fire hazard because the blast wave would arrive after the heat flash had passed, except in the central area of complete destruction where the heat flash would not be the predominant effect.

5.13 Because buildings have a considerable shielding effect on one another in a closely built up area the windows of the upper floors are more important than those lower down.

5.14 Blast damage, the scattering of domestic fires, the rupture of gas pipes or short-circuiting of electrical wiring may start secondary fires. The risk of these fires would be reduced by extinguishing boilers and open-fires and by turning off gas and electricity at the mains.

The possibilities of a fire storm

5.15 The chief feature of a fire storm is the generation of high winds which are drawn into the centre of the fire area to feed the flames. These in-rushing winds prevent the spread of the fires outwards but ensure almost complete destruction by fire of everything within the affected area. A fire storm inevitably increases the number of casualties since it becomes impossible for people to escape by their own efforts and they succumb to the effects of suffocation and heat stroke.

5.16 In the last war fire storms were caused in the old city of Hamburg as a result of heavy incendiary attacks and at Hiroshima but not Nagasaki. A close study of these fire storms and of German cities in which fire storms did not occur revealed several interesting features. A fire storm occurred only in an area of several square miles, heavily built-up with buildings containing plenty of combustible material and where at least every other building in the area had been set alight by incendiary attack.

5.17 It is considered unlikely that an initial density of fires, equivalent to one in every other building, would be started by a nuclear explosion over a British city; studies have shown that due to shielding a much smaller proportion of buildings than this would be exposed to heat flash. Moreover, the buildings in the centres of most British cities are now of fire-resistant construction and more widely spaced than 30–40 years ago. Fire storms after nuclear attack are therefore unlikely in British cities but the possibility would be greatly reduced by the control of small initial and secondary fires.

6 Crater Formation and Ground Shock

Introduction

6.1 When a nuclear detonation takes place on or near the ground, an appreciable amount of the energy generated is expended in making a crater and, at the same time, a shock wave is transmitted outwards through the ground. A description of the effects of bursts in or near water is given in paragraphs 1.19 and 1.20.

Crater formation

6.2 In a surface burst a considerable quantity of vaporised or pulverised material is sucked up by the ascending fireball and associated air currents. A still larger quantity is gouged out of the ground by the force of the explosion and is deposited around the crater to add to the 'lip' formed by the ground which is compressed and forced up round the perimeter. This combined lip has a width roughly equal to the radius of the crater and a height of about a quarter of the depth of the crater.

6.3 The dimensions of craters produced by nuclear weapons of different powers when detonated on saturated clay are shown in Table 8. The craters are slightly deeper but less extensive on dry soil or hard rock and appropriate conversion factors are given below that Table. Scaling laws for crater dimensions and a formula for calculating the total volume of a crater are to be found in Appendix II, paragraph 2.

Table 8   Crater dimensions (in feet) for a ground burst on saturated clay

Weapon power	20 KT	100 KT	½ MT	1 MT	2 MT	5 MT	10 MT	20 MT
Radius of crater (a)	300	510	850	1,100	1,360	1,700	2,200	2,800
Radius of crater lip (a)	600	1,020	1,700	2,200	2,720	3,400	4,400	5,600
Depth of crater (b)	40	55	80	100	120	150	180	210

(a) To get ranges (radii) in dry soil, divide by 1.7
(b) To get depths in dry soil, divide by 0.7
(a) To get ranges (radii) in hard rock, divide by 2
(b) To get depths in hard rock, divide by 0.9

6.4 Since British rivers have relatively small flows, catchment and flood plain areas, it is unlikely that the flooding caused by craters in rivers would extend beyond the area of complete destruction. In any case, the radioactivity in the vicinity of the crater would be so intense that no works, such as cutting a channel through the crater lip, would be possible for a considerable time after the detonation.

Ground shock

6.5 The ground shock effects produced by a megaton surface burst are similar to those produced by an earthquake of moderate intensity, but the pressure in the ground shock-wave decreases more rapidly with distance. The shock effects on structures above ground are irrelevant, since they do not occur beyond the distances at which these structures are totally destroyed by blast. Its effects on structures below ground depend upon the ability of the structure to accommodate itself to the accompanying ground movement. Damage would vary according to the depth below ground, the type of soil, its moisture content and the duration of the blast wave. Thus, small self-contained structures should move bodily with the surrounding ground and should be undamaged beyond 2 or 3 crater radii from the burst. Equally so, long flexible underground structures, such as pipes, should be able to accommodate themselves to the comparatively small ground movement and should be undamaged outside about 3 crater radii, say, under $1\frac{1}{2}$ miles for a 10 MT bomb.

7 Effects of Damage from Air Blast

Introduction

7.1 The enormous pressure produced in the detonation of a nuclear weapon gives a violent push to the surrounding air with the result that a wave of high pressure is transmitted outwards through the air; in addition, a strong wind is caused by the bulk movement of the air. The pressure wave is followed by a suction wave, creating a partial vacuum which in turn causes a wind in the reverse direction towards ground zero.

7.2 Initially, the pressure wave is transmitted at a speed considerably greater than that of sound (which is about 1,100 ft per second) but it gradually slows down to this speed. Its speed also depends upon the temperature of the air through which it is transmitted and this factor gives rise to the shock wave. When the front part of the wave reaches a particular point, the air at that point is compressed and heated and the rear portion of the wave is able to move faster through the hot air. Eventually it catches up with the front part. The wave front then becomes steeper and almost vertical as illustrated in Figure 1.

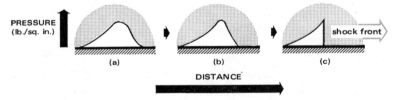

Figure 1   Simplified representation of development of shock front

Any obstacle in its path would experience a sharp blow due to the very sudden rise from atmospheric pressure to the peak pressure of the wave front.

7.3 Shock waves can be reflected from surfaces. When this happens the peak pressure on the surface of the obstacle may be increased by a factor between 2 and 8 depending upon the strength of the original shock wave. The degree of damage to buildings may be related to the initial blow from the shock pressure alone or to the combined effects of the duration of the shock wave and the peak shock pressure.

Mach wave

7.4 A special way in which a shock wave, travelling outwards along the ground, may be intensified is known as the MACH effect, which occurs when the blast wave from an air burst strikes and is reflected from the ground as illustrated in Figure 2. The reflected wave also moves outwards through air heated by the direct shock wave. It will catch up with the latter at some distance from ground zero to form a MACH wave in which the peak pressure is almost double that of the original shock wave.

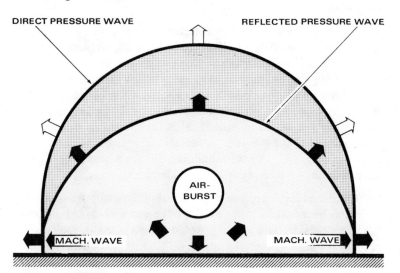

Figure 2   Formation of Mach Wave

Structural damage

7.5 Damage to a structure depends upon the power of the bomb, whether it is air or ground burst and the distance of the structure from the detonation. In addition the amount of damage will be governed by the type and strength of the structure, its size, shape and orientation with respect to the explosion and the location of potential openings, such as doors, windows and panels which could fail during the passage of the blast wave. The damage is the result of displacement by two major forces exerted by the blast; first the abrupt rise in pressure as the shock wave hits the building and passes over it in a fraction of a second and, second, the drag force which is exerted by the high wind throughout the duration of the positive pressure wave

31

and which tends to distort the building or to push it over on its side.

Shock or diffraction loading on a building

7.6 When the front of a shock wave strikes a building it is reflected and the pressure on the face towards the explosion is momentarily increased by a factor of two or more. As the main shock front moves over and around the building, the pressure on that face falls rapidly to the normal peak pressure before reflection occurred, and this same pressure is exerted side-on to the building. The shock front then bends round the opposite end until the whole building is engulfed in the blast wave and the same pressure is exerted on all four walls and on the roof.

7.7 Before the blast wave has completely surrounded the building, there will be a considerable difference between the pressure on the side facing and that on the opposite side away from the explosion and, consequently, the building tends to move bodily in the same direction as the blast wave. If the building has relatively few openings, say less than 5 per cent of the surface area, it will be subjected to this lateral loading for the length of time it takes for the shock front to pass from one end of the building to the other. For example, if the shock front has to pass 75 ft over a building, the force would operate for about a tenth of a second causing considerable damage.

7.8 After the blast wave has engulfed a building with few openings, there may be insufficient time for the air pressure inside to build up to the value outside. The building would be subjected to the crushing effect of the higher external pressure on the roof and on all four walls for the duration of the positive pressure wave. This period is several seconds in the case of megaton weapons at the limit for complete destruction.

7.9 In buildings with a greater percentage of openings, equalisation of pressure will occur fairly quickly and, because of reflections, the pressure inside may build up until it exceeds the external pressure. This may lead to the building exploding outwards, since buildings are not normally designed to withstand abnormal internal pressures. This explosion effect, which is common in hurricanes and has been observed in atomic tests, could be typical in British houses at the limiting distances for total destruction (Plates 2 to 6).

7.10 Throughout the duration of the positive pressure wave, wind drag forces act on objects and structural elements which, because of their small size or cross-section, allow rapid equalisation of pressure

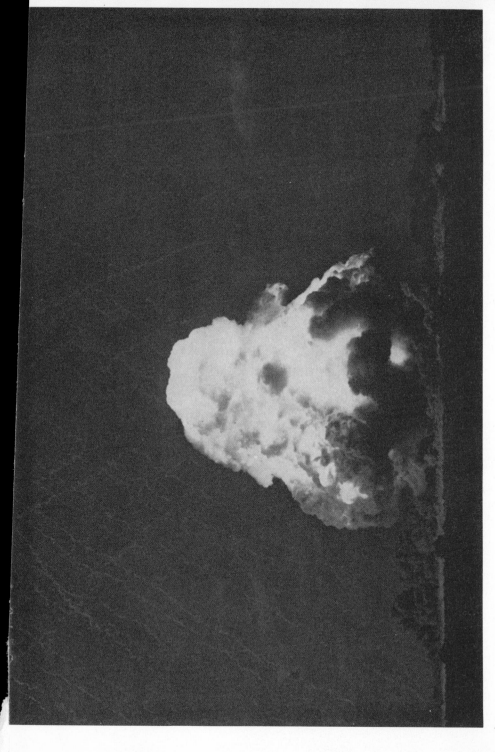

Plate 1   The Fireball

Plate 2   House at 1 mile from ground zero — Before

Plate 3   The same house at the moment of explosion (1)

Plate 4   The heat effect (2)

Plate 5   The blast effect (3)

Plate 6   The end result (4)

round them. These objects are not so vulnerable to an all-round external pressure. Drag forces, for example, shift small objects such as bricks, broken tiles and glass from damaged buildings. They damage open-girder bridges, pylons and trees. (See also paragraph 7.13 for effects on human beings.)

Ranges of damage to typical British houses and of road blockage

7.11 Table 9 shows the ranges of various categories of damage and street blockage for ground burst weapons of different powers. It is estimated that slight damage to typical British houses would occur when the static overpressure in the shock front was about 0.75 pounds per square inch; the houses would need repairs to remain habitable at 1.5 psi and they would be irreparably damaged at about 6 psi.

Table 9 Average ranges of blast damage to typical British houses and blockage of streets. Ground burst nuclear weapons: ranges in miles

Weapon power	20 KT	100 KT	½ MT	1 MT	2 MT	5 MT	10 MT	20 MT
Damage ring 'A' Houses totally destroyed, streets impassable	0–⅜	0–¾	0–1¼	0–1½	0–2	0–2¾	0–3½	0–4½
Damage ring 'B' Houses irreparably damaged, streets blocked until cleared with mechanical aids	⅜–⅝	¾–1	1¼–1¾	1½–2¼	2–3	2¾–4	3½–5	4½–6¼
Damage ring 'C' Houses severely to moderately damaged: progress in streets made difficult by debris	⅝–1⅝	1–2¾	1¾–4½	2¼–5½	3–7	4–10	5–12	6¼–15½
Damage ring 'D' Houses lightly damaged, streets open but some glass and tile debris	1⅝–2½	2¾–4¼	4½–7¼	6–9	7–12	10–16	12–20	15½–25

Effects on bridges

7.12 As noted in paragraph 7.10, wind drag is the main cause of damage to open girder bridges, though these bridges may also be lifted bodily and moved from their abutments as a result of blast reflection from the ground or water underneath them. Table 10 shows the expected ranges at which bridges would collapse from the effects of ground burst bombs.

Table 10 Bridge collapse from ground burst nuclear weapons. (*Ranges in miles from ground zero*)

Weapon power	20 KT	100 KT	½ MT	1 MT	2 MT	5 MT	10 MT	20 MT
Steel truss	½	1	1½	2	2½	3¼	4	5¼
Heavy masonry or concrete	¼	⅓	⅝	¾	1	1¼	1½	2

Effects on human beings

7.13 Experience in World War II showed that the human body is surprisingly resistant to blast pressure, and that the more likely sources of bodily injury are being hurled against obstacles or being struck by potentially lethal projectiles. With nuclear weapons, it seems that the lethal blast pressure may be considerably less than it is for high explosive blast, because of the longer duration of the blast. This increase in duration, however, also increases the effects of the drag forces, and the predominant risk from blast will be from the latter effects. For example, if a man were exposed to the blast of a 10 MT bomb: to be killed by direct blast pressure, he would have to be within about 2 miles of GZ. Yet, if he were standing in the open anywhere within 5 or 6 miles of GZ, he would be carried along by the wind drag forces and could strike an obstacle hard enough for the impact to be lethal. If he were lying on the ground, the man might be able to avoid this translational effect, but even out to, say, 10 miles, he could be exposed to lethal missiles carried by the blast wind. This hazard would apply also to people in their houses when windows, roofs and doors were damaged by blast.

Effects on vehicles

7.14 Cars and buses with their windows closed would be liable to be crushed by external blast pressure, but the more serious hazard is being blown over by the drag forces arising from the blast wind. The estimated ranges of severe displacement of motor vehicles are given in Table 11.

Table 11 Motor vehicle damage from ground burst nuclear weapons. (*Ranges in miles from ground zero*)

Weapon power	20 KT	100 KT	½ MT	1 MT	2 MT	5 MT	10 MT	20 MT
Severe displacement of motor vehicles at	¾	1¼	2¼	2¾	3½	4¾	6	7½

Effects on public utility services

7.15 Except near the crater (see paragraph 6.5) the effect of a nuclear detonation on public utility services would probably be confined to damage above ground, say, to poles and pylons carrying overhead telephone and power lines. Damage to delicate equipment in the exchanges would cause disruption of the telephone service out to ranges corresponding to those for moderate damage to houses (see Table 9). Installations such as gas terminals, distribution points and water pumping stations, electricity generating stations and sub-stations would suffer structural damage. Underground services such as water and gas mains would probably be undamaged unless near the crater, but the pipe connections would often be ruptured in damaged buildings some distance away.

The debris problem

7.16 It will be seen from Table 9 that the problem of access would be a serious one in built-up areas. Even without the radiation hazard, movement of vehicular traffic might be seriously restricted or halted over wide areas until the debris is cleared. Wide streets, streets with front gardens and routes radial to the point of burst are less likely to be blocked to the same degree and might be given priority for clearance.

7.17 Trees are very vulnerable to long duration blast and in many cases fallen trees would block roads at a greater distance from ground zero than any other type of debris. The estimated distances for trees in leaf damaged by ground burst bombs are given in Table 12.

Table 12   Tree damage from ground burst nuclear weapons. (Ranges in miles from ground zero)

Weapon power	20 KT	100 KT	$\frac{1}{2}$ MT	1 MT	2 MT	5 MT	10 MT	20 MT
Trees								
90% blown down	1	$1\frac{3}{4}$	3	$3\frac{3}{4}$	$4\frac{3}{4}$	$6\frac{1}{4}$	8	10
30% blown down	$1\frac{1}{4}$	$2\frac{1}{4}$	$3\frac{3}{4}$	$4\frac{1}{2}$	6	$7\frac{3}{4}$	10	$12\frac{1}{2}$
Branch damage	$1\frac{3}{4}$	3	5	$6\frac{1}{4}$	8	$10\frac{1}{2}$	14	17

Relation between blast effects of air and ground burst weapons

7.18 As noted in paragraph 1.22, the range of blast damage is substantially greater from an air burst than from a ground burst weapon. For practical purposes it can be assumed that the ranges of the various categories of damage for ground burst bombs shown in Tables 9 to 12 would be increased by 30 per cent if the same sized weapon were air burst near the optimum height.

8 Effects of Residual Radiation from Fallout

Introduction

8.1 The radioactive fission products from a nuclear weapon, burst on or near the ground, would condense on the debris and dust raised by the force of the explosion. They would be deposited around the crater and dropped more slowly from the cloud over a broad area which might extend several hundred miles downwind.

8.2 Particles measuring between one-fiftieth of a millimetre and half a millimetre would be deposited over a wide area in a complex pattern of radioactive fallout, the shape and extent of which would be determined by the wind strength and directions at the various atmospheric levels through which these particles fall. With the average winds in the United Kingdom the fallout pattern might extend to several hundred miles downwind of ground zero. The radioactivity of the fission products would decay in accordance with the formula in paragraph 3.4.

8.3 Particles of less than one-fiftieth of a millimetre would be carried by the wind to much greater distances and might not be deposited on the ground for weeks, or indeed for several years if they had been carried into the stratosphere. By that time the radioactivity would have decayed several thousand-fold and the individual particles would have become so widely dispersed in the atmosphere that they would no longer represent a significant fallout hazard when finally deposited.

The different hazards presented by fallout

8.4 There are many ways in which heavy fissile atoms can split into two not quite equal parts, and consequently fission products consist of some 200 different types of atomic nuclei or isotopes of about 35 elements (see paragraph 3.4).

8.5 These radioactive isotopes are unstable and tend to disintegrate or decay in one or more stages, by emitting one or more of the following:

a. alpha particles which are four times as heavy as hydrogen atoms and lose all their energy by collision with other atoms in passing through a few inches of air; they cannot penetrate clothing or unbroken skin;

b. beta particles which are high-speed electrons or negative charges of electricity stopped by air within 2 to 12 yards, depending on the energy with which they are expelled from a nucleus: they are unable to penetrate deeply beneath clothing and skin but they may cause skin burns;

c. gamma rays which are forms of electromagnetic radiation like light and heat and which travel with the speed of light: in air they can reach distances of many hundreds or even thousands of feet before they are stopped by the atoms of oxygen and nitrogen in the atmosphere; like X-rays they can penetrate, but more readily, through the deeper tissues and organs of the body.

8.6 It should now be clear that radioactive fallout presents two separate hazards:

a. contact for, say, 8 hours or more with, or close proximity to, the skin or organs within the body. This hazard is caused by fallout on clothing, on the skin and hair, and inside the body through cuts or the mouth and digestive system.

b. gamma radiation, from fallout deposited over a wide area which affects the whole body.

8.7 An indication of the level of beta contamination (which is the main source of the contact hazard) is obtained by the use of a survey meter very close to the suspected surface. The survey meter has a window flap which, when open, allows beta and gamma radiation to enter and, when closed, excludes the beta. The difference between the two readings gives an indication of the level of beta contamination. The environmental gamma dose is usually measured by holding the survey meter 3 feet above a contaminated surface and taking a reading with the flap closed.

Detection and warning of fallout

8.8 Particles may be seen coming down or may be visible as dust on some surfaces. However, the human senses are incapable of identifying nuclear radiation and consequently instruments are required to detect and measure it. When warning of imminent fallout has been given, the public should take the best available all-round cover from gamma radiation for at least one week and possibly for two weeks. It would be necessary to remain under cover until the intensity of the gamma radiation in the area could be monitored and until it had decayed sufficiently to permit outdoor exposure for limited periods. While under cover the prospects of survival would be enhanced by having a supply of drinking water, some food and primitive sanitary facilities.

Relation between distance from nearest fallout and total dose

8.9 Figure 3 shows the proportion of the total radiation dose which a man would receive at various distances if he were standing on ground evenly contaminated with fallout. It will be observed that half of the total dose would come from within a circle roughly of a radius of 25 feet around him. This radius would be greater on very smooth ground and less on rough and uneven ground.

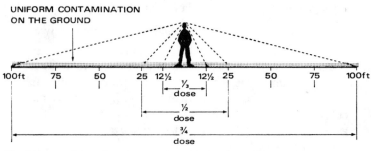

Figure 3   Total dose from fallout—contribution from different distances

Relation between the external radiation hazard and the hazard from breathing or swallowing fallout particles

8.10 When fallout is coming down, or in an area already covered by radioactive fallout, the gamma radiation hazard from the surroundings would be far greater than the hazard from any radioactive dust which might be inhaled or swallowed. Protection is afforded by being inside behind the thickest available walls and as far below the roof as possible (see paragraphs 1.31, 9.2 and 9.3). In multi-storey buildings the top two floors should be avoided. Nevertheless, the contact hazard would be minimised by removing radioactive fallout from the skin, hair and clothing as soon as this was practicable.

8.11 Ordinary headgear, clothing, boots and gloves keep fallout and the alpha and beta particles away from the body and give temporary protection against the contact hazard, but if contaminated, especially with wet or muddy fallout, they should be removed or replaced at the earliest opportunity. They do not provide any significant protection against gamma radiation.

38

Fallout patterns and dose-rate contours

8.12 Fallout areas in the United Kingdom would probably have an irregular shape in customary weather conditions. There are two main reasons for this; first, particles of different sizes fall at different rates from all parts of the very extensive cloud. For example, a particle one millimetre in diameter falls from 60,000 ft in about 15 minutes compared with about 20 hours for a particle 20 times smaller. Secondly, the falling particles are carried along by the winds at different speeds and directions at different heights.

8.13 The dose-rate would increase towards the centre of the fallout area and lines could be drawn through points which receive simultaneously equal dose-rates. These isodose-rate contours and the spacing between them at different places may be quite irregular and may include several 'hot' areas or plateaux caused by local topography, air turbulence or rain showers. Figure 4 illustrates the fallout pattern and contours after a ground burst in the megaton range.

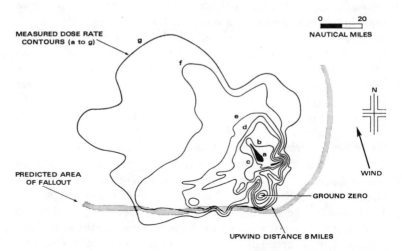

Figure 4   Comparison of fallout prediction with test results: Contour values: Reference dose-rate at one Hour, in rph (see paragraph 8.15). a. 2,500; b. 1,000; c. 500; d. 250; e. 100; f. 50; g. 25.

Taken from the US Congress Publication 'The nature of radioactive fallout and its effect on man' (Hearings before the Special Sub-committee on Radiation, 27 May to 3 June 1957) Part I, pages 304 and 305.

8.14 Since fission products decay rapidly at first and then at a progressively decreasing rate represented by formulae such as the $t^{-1 \cdot 2}$ decay law or the seven-tenths rule (see paragraphs 3.4 and 3.5), the fallout pattern on the ground would be contracting as it formed. Initial fallout, close to the damaged area, might be all down in one or two hours after the detonation whereas 200 miles downwind, assuming a mean wind of 20 miles per hour, it would not start to come down for another 8 hours and it might continue to do so for a further 10 to 15 hours, by which time it would have decayed by a factor of between 20 and 30 compared with the earlier fallout.

Standard reference time for dose-rate contours

8.15 It is clear that a standard reference time is needed to define a consistent set of fallout contours and to enable the dose-rates at any place within the pattern to be calculated at any other desired time. For home defence purposes, it is convenient to choose as the standard reference time either one hour (H+1) or seven hours (H+7) after the detonation. In practice dose-rates would be measured and reported together with the times and positions as soon as maximum readings had been reached. From the decay law these dose-rates could then be converted to the dose-rate corresponding to the standard reference time. In this way, a pattern of one-hour (DR1) or seven-hour (DR7) reference dose-rate contours could be built up on a map as the fallout front advanced over the country; from this pattern, it would be possible to estimate what the dose-rates would be at any particular place and subsequent time, after the fallout had come down. Further fallout would affect the pattern. Essential operations could then be planned and public control exercised in the light of this information.

Relation between bomb power and contour areas

8.16 Aerial and ground surveys of the fallout at weapon trials have shown that about two-thirds of the total fission product activity from a surface burst is deposited in a day or two within the fallout pattern. In comparing the fallout patterns from weapons of two different powers, it has been found that the areas lying within the same dose-rate contour are approximately proportional to the yield of the two weapons, provided they have the same percentage fission yield. For example, the area enclosed by the 10 rph DR1 contour from a 5 MT 100 per cent fission explosion is 10 times larger than that enclosed by the same contour from a $\frac{1}{2}$ MT 100 per cent fission explosion (see scaling laws in Appendix II). While this relationship holds very roughly, within a factor of two either way, for downwind contour areas, the contamination pattern upwind and crosswind from ground zero is more complex and cannot be adequately described by such simple scaling laws. This is not unexpected as the upwind contaminated area will be a much smaller part of the total fallout pattern.

Downwind areas covered by fallout

8.17 Table 13 shows the approximate size of areas covered by a series of reference dose-rate contours one hour after surface bursts of weapons ranging from 20 KT to 20 MT in power. In other fallout patterns the relationship between high and low dose-rate areas may vary considerably from the figures in Table 13. Since the distribution of fallout from a MT weapon would depend mainly on the cloud dimensions and height, roughly the same area would be covered by fallout irrespective of its fission yield but the dose-rate at any particular locality would be proportional to the per cent fission yield. For example, to convert from 50 per cent to say 60 per cent fission yield over the same contour area, the dose-rates (DR1's) would now have to be multiplied by the factor $\frac{60}{50}$. A re-plot of DR1 values against area would enable areas to be read off corresponding to the DR1 contour values in Table 13.

Table 13   Downwind Contamination. Areas of contours for reference dose-rates at one hour after burst (DR1's) assuming 50% fission yield for $\frac{1}{4}$ MT and larger weapons and 100% for KT weapons

Reference contour dose-rate rph at *one* hour after burst (DR1's) in rph	Areas in square miles for weapon power							
	20 KT	100 KT	$\frac{1}{4}$ MT	1 MT	2 MT	5 MT	10 MT	20 MT
3000	0.2	1.2	10	20	40	100	200	400
1000	1.3	6.4	45	90	190	500	900	1,900
300	5	25	200	300	700	2,000	3,500	7,000
100	16	82	450	900	2,000	5,000	9,000	18,000
30	50	250	1,100	2,000	4,000	11,000	22,000	44,000
10	200	1,000	2,250	4,500	9,000	24,000	47,000	93,000

8.18 The time between the first arrival of fallout and maximum dose-rate may be anything between one quarter and 4 times that between detonation and the first arrival of fallout: it may be several hours after the maximum dose-rate is reached before fallout ceases.

8.19 Table 13 shows that people in large areas of the United Kingdom could be exposed in the open to dangerous and, in many cases, lethal residual radiation. For example, the 300 rph one-hour reference contour (DR1) from a 1 MT ground burst (50 per cent fission) would cover an area of roughly 300 square miles and might extend 50 miles downwind. At the extreme downwind edge of this contour, fallout might start about 2 hours after the detonation and a dangerous dose of about 600r could be accumulated by 48 hours after the burst. In a small part of the total area of 300 square miles the external dose-rate might be so high that people would suffer from radiation sickness after a few days even when protected in buildings.

Upwind and crosswind contamination in the damaged area

8.20 Samples of radioactive particles collected by rockets and aircraft from known points within the stabilised clouds have led to the concept of two cloud models:

i. for weapons of less than 100 KT, the cloud is roughly spherical with a uniform distribution of radioactive particles;

ii. for weapons of 100 KT and above the cloud is shaped like a mushroom—a larger cylindrical disc on top of a cylindrical stem. The size of the cloud as well as the heights of its top and base will, of course, depend upon the weapon power (see Appendix II, Table 26). Activity appears to be concentrated in the upper part of the stem and in the central and lower sections of the disc.

8.21 The cloud from a 1 MT detonation takes about 7 minutes to reach an altitude of 60,000 ft and become stable. After that, the largest particles (about 1 millimetre), which are concentrated at the top of the stem, take about 40 minutes to fall. Particles of about 500 micrometres (half the previous size) are concentrated in the inner half of the radius of the disc and fall in 80 minutes; while the particles at the edge of the disc are predominantly less than 250 micrometres and fall in about 3 hours.

8.22 In the absence of wind at any level up to cloud height (a very rare occurrence in the UK) the cloud models predict a circular fallout pattern around ground zero, with the same radius as the cloud. For example, the radius is 29 miles for a 10 MT detonation (see Appendix II, Table 26). With a 15 mile per hour mean wind in the same direction at all relevant heights, the 500-micrometre particles in the cloud from a 10 MT bomb would extend out to 15 miles from the cloud centre and would take about 80 minutes to be deposited on the ground. A 250-micrometre particle falling from the extreme upwind edge of the cloud after 3 hours would be deposited on the ground (45–29) 16 miles downwind of ground zero and smaller particles would fall still further downwind.

8.23 The cloud model for the larger weapons indicates that very little fallout is likely to be deposited upwind beyond the limit of complete destruction, unless the winds at all levels up to cloud height are of exceptionally low speed or are in opposite directions at different levels. Around the upwind half of the damaged area the extent and intensity of radioactive fallout will also depend upon weather conditions at the time. It is possible that there may be no fallout upwind beyond the range of complete destruction. For planning purposes Table 14 has been included to show upwind distances of a series of 1-hour reference contours from a large megaton weapon for two possible patterns of fallout under low and moderate wind conditions respectively.

Table 14   Contamination upwind in the damaged area (10 MT). Upwind distances from GZ to 1-hour reference contours (DRI's) for two possible fallout patterns

Dose-rate at 1-hour after burst (DR1) rph	Upwind distance (miles) for mean winds of	
	5 mph	15 mph
0.3	21	7
1.0	16	5
3	11	4
10	7	2
30	4	in crater
100	2	in crater
300	in crater	in crater

8.24 On the flanks of the damaged and contaminated area, the contour for any given dose-rate will extend further crosswind from ground zero than directly upwind, but considerably less than the downwind extension. There is no simple method of estimating crosswind distances.

9 Protection Against Gamma Radiation from Fallout

Introduction

9.1 This chapter describes a method which has been devised for assessing the protection afforded by dwelling houses and other buildings against gamma radiation from fallout, based on the dimensions of the buildings and the weight of the material used in their construction. The method ignores a number of factors; such as buildings of irregular shape and the proportion of wall area consisting of thin wall panels, windows and doors. However it does enable a reasonable estimate to be made of the protection obtainable in certain types of dwelling house which are common in the United Kingdom. A higher degree of protection is afforded by lower, middle and inner parts of larger buildings, such as office blocks and flats, than the upper and outer parts.

9.2 Gamma radiation can penetrate all material but the intensity of radiation passing through any material is progressively reduced and, if the material is sufficiently thick, it affords adequate protection. The protection afforded increases with the weight of material which lies between the sources and the subjects in question. For example 9 inches of brickwork or 7 inches of concrete will reduce the dose-rate to about one-tenth of the original rate.

9.3 The gamma dose-rate which a person receives depends also on his distance from a source of radiation; from a point source (and fallout is not a single point source) it is inversely proportional to the square of the distance. For example doubling the distance gives a four-fold reduction in dose-rate. In practice, thickness and heaviness of the walls are usually more significant than the size of the building and, hence, the distance of the subject from the source.

9.4 A building therefore affords protection in two ways according to its size and the position of its occupants. Firstly, it keeps the radioactive fallout at a distance and reduces the dose-rate from the individual particles in inverse proportion to the square of this distance and, secondly, the weight of the walls, upper floors and roof themselves reduce the dose-rate. The more massive the building is, the greater its degree of protection. Surrounding buildings increase the protection afforded by an otherwise isolated building.

Protective factors of buildings and houses

9.5 The protection afforded by a building against the gamma radiation from fallout is expressed as the 'protective factor' (PF) of the building; that is the factor by which the dose-rate received by a person in the building is reduced as compared roughly with that received by a person standing on smooth flat ground in the open. Thus, if a particular building has a protective factor of 100 it means that the dose-rate for a person in the building is 1/100th of the dose-rate he would be receiving in the open.

9.6 The protective factor will vary in even a simple rectangular building, it will be greatest at positions shielded by upper floors or internal walls and lowest near windows, doors or the thinner parts of the external wall. Allowance cannot easily be made for these variations. The protective factor at 3 ft above the mid-point of the floor level of the building is assumed to hold good for the whole of that floor level. Few buildings are of a simple rectangular shape and it is not feasible to take into account all the irregularities. For practical purposes the average length and breadth of the building is used in calculations. The method of dealing with parts of buildings is described in paragraph 9.15.

9.7 The degrees of protection afforded by the thickness and the density of the materials, of which the walls, floor and roof are constructed, are combined and expressed in terms of the weight per square foot.

9.8 In practice, the walls and floors of a building are seldom of uniform thickness throughout; walls are thickened in places by buttresses and chimney breasts and floors by beams. Variations of this sort are averaged; for example, in the case of a beam and slab floor, the total weight of the beams and slabs is divided by the area of the floor. Precise weights of wall, floor and roof material may be difficult to obtain but structural engineers and quantity surveyors would be able to estimate these weights with an accuracy which is more than adequate for the purpose of these calculations. Weights per square foot of area and, where appropriate, for each inch of thickness of some common building materials are given in Table 15.

9.9 Where it is necessary to block external openings in order to provide sufficient protection, protective factors should be calculated

Table 15   Weights per square foot of some common building materials

Brickwork	per inch thickness			10 lb
Stone	,,	,,	,,	12 lb
Reinforced concrete	,,	,,	,,	12 lb
Asphalt	,,	,,	,,	12 lb
Hollow tile	,,	,,	,,	8 lb
Plaster	,,	,,	,,	8 lb
Boards	,,	,,	,,	4 lb
Tiles				14–18 lb
Slates				8 lb
Corrugated asbestos cement sheets				3½ lb
Corrugated steel sheets				2–3 lb

on the assumption that the blocking material has the same weight in lb per square foot as the wall area.

Shielding against residual gamma radiation: half value thickness of shielding materials

9.10 The thickness of material needed to reduce the dose-rate in a beam of gamma rays by half is called the half-value thickness of that particular material. This is illustrated in Figure 5 for residual gamma radiation through concrete. Each successive 'half value' layer similarly reduces the dose transmitted by half for weights up to about 140 lb per square foot.

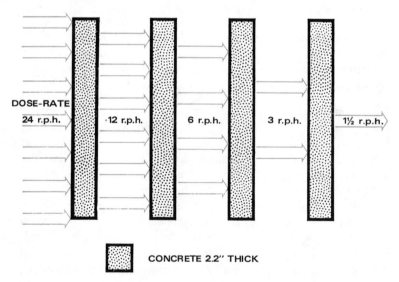

DOSE-RATE

24 r.p.h.   ·12 r.p.h.   6 r.p.h.   3 r.p.h.   1½ r.p.h.

CONCRETE 2.2″ THICK

Figure 5   Diagrammatic illustration of the reduction of residual gamma radiation intensity by successive 2.2 inch half-value layers of concrete or equivalent material.

9.11 Table 16 shows the half-value thickness for common materials of construction against residual radiation from fallout.

Table 16   Half-value thicknesses of shielding materials against residual radiation

Material	Slab density in lbs per square foot for one inch of thickness	Half value thickness (inches)
Steel	41	0.7
Concrete	12	2.2
Brickwork	10	2.8
Earth	8	3.3

Thus a 2.2 in. thickness of concrete will reduce the dose of residual radiation to one-half of its original value, 4.4 in. will reduce it to a quarter, 6.6 in. to one-eighth and so on. Brick walls 4½, 9 and 13½ in. thick will reduce the intensity of residual radiation by factors of 3, 10 and 30 respectively. For thicker and larger shields the contribution from penetrating scattered radiation increases, therefore the reduction factor is slightly less for the thicker shields than the successive half-value thickness formula would indicate.

Method of calculating protective factors

9.12 External radiation can be regarded as entering the building from five directions, namely, through the roof and through each of the four walls: this is equivalent to five separate sources each of which contributes, by addition, to the total radiation intensity inside. Each of these separate contributions can be conveniently expressed as a percentage of what the intensity outside would be at 3 ft above smooth flat ground. Tables 17 and 18 enable the contributions to this total percentage to be calculated for the roof and for each wall. Tables 19 and 22 show various correction factors. The contributions are added to give the total percentage; 100 divided by this total is taken to be the protective factor for the building.

9.13 In calculating protective factors it is assumed that:

a. the radioactive fallout matter is uniformly deposited on the ground and on the roof, the roof is flat with the same overall length and breadth as the external walls of the building, and the height of the building is the average height of the actual roof between the eaves and the ridge;

b. there is no deposit on the walls, window-sills or any projections from the walls; and

c. no radioactive material entered the building.

Roof contribution

9.14 To find the roof contribution, the first step is to calculate the value of $\dfrac{\sqrt{A}}{H-3}$, where A is the area of the room in square feet and H is the height in feet of the average roof level above the floor. The next step is to estimate the weight of overhead material (roof and upper floors) in pounds per square foot of floor area. The roof contribution may then be read from Table 17. Thus if the area is 900 square feet and the height is 25 feet we have $\dfrac{\sqrt{A}}{H-3} = \dfrac{30}{22} = 1.4$. If the weight of the overhead material is 40 pounds per square foot, we find from Table 17 by interpolation that the roof contribution is 2.7 per cent.

Buildings sub-divided by internal walls

9.15 Some buildings have substantial internal walls unlike the thin partitions of normal domestic architecture. Flats, maisonettes and office blocks may be examples where such internal walls may modify the contribution of radiation from the roof. A simple approximation may be made as follows for the effect of substantial internal walls on the roof contribution:

Provided the partition walls extend right up to roof level and are of 45 pounds or more per square foot (for example, thicker than $4\frac{1}{2}$ inch brickwork) then the roof area is taken as that obtained by measurement up to such partitions.

Contribution through walls to rooms above ground

9.16 The contribution through each wall can be found from Table 18 using the value of $\sqrt{A}$ obtained in paragraph 9.14 and the weight of the wall or walls on each of the four sides of the room. The table gives the contribution to the total radiation through each wall to the mid-point of the area being considered. Thus if the area is 400 square feet and the wall on one side is 100 pounds per square foot then the contribution through that wall is 2.2 per cent. This value is subject to one or more corrections as follows:

i. The correction factor for long narrow buildings is obtained by measuring the length and breadth of the building (up to main partition walls as explained in paragraph 9.15). Then, if L is the length of the wall being considered and P the perimeter of the building, the correction factor is $\dfrac{4L}{P}$. Thus if we have a building measuring 40 feet by 10 feet and the walls are 100 pounds per square foot then the basic contribution through each of the walls from Table 18 is 2.2 per cent. The correction factor for each of the two longer walls will be $\dfrac{4 \times 40}{100} = 1.6$ and for each of the two shorter walls $\dfrac{4 \times 10}{100} = 0.4$. Thus the corrected contributions for the four walls would be $2.2 \times 1.6 = 3.52$ per cent for each of the longer walls and $2.2 \times 0.4 = 0.88$ per cent for each of the two shorter walls.

ii.   The correction factor in parts of the building above the ground can be obtained directly from Table 19, using the height of the floor above the outside ground level. For buildings on steeply sloping ground this correction factor will vary from wall to wall and the average height of the floor above the ground should be used for each wall.

iii.   A rough correction for shielding from other buildings may be applied as follows:

For buildings of at least the same size up to 30 feet away from the wall being considered, the contribution through that wall is reduced to about one half of the uncorrected value.

For buildings between 30 and 80 feet away from the wall being considered, the contribution through that wall is reduced to three quarters of the uncorrected value. This should be applied only when the shielding wall is about one and a half times as long as the shielded wall. If this condition does not apply then the shielding effect should be ignored, as should the effect of buildings more than 80 feet away.

Scattered contribution from walls to rooms below ground
9.17 The scattered contribution from each wall to rooms below the ground can be obtained from Table 20 using the value of $\sqrt{A}$ as obtained in paragraph 9.14, and the weight of the walls in pounds per square foot. The Table gives the contribution scattered through the wall being considered to the midpoint of a basement room. Thus if the area is 400 square feet and the wall on one side of the ground is 100 pounds per square foot, then the contribution through that wall to the basement room is 0.22 per cent.

This value is subject to multiplication by correction factors as follows:

i.   For long and narrow buildings, as calculated in paragraph 9.16(i).

ii. For shielding from other buildings as calculated in paragraph 9.16(iii).

iii. For depth of basement, obtained directly from Table 21, using the depth of the basement floor below ground level and the floor area of the building in square feet.

iv. For the attenuation due to the basement ceiling, obtained directly from Table 22, using the figure for the weight of the ceiling (or ceilings if a double basement) in pounds per square ft.

Example of Calculation of Protective Factor

9.18 For this purpose consideration is given to a two-storey building above a basement, of the following dimensions:

1. The building is detached and measures 60 feet by 30 feet.

2. The weight of the outside walls is 90 pounds per square foot (say, 9 inches of brickwork).

3. The height of the rooms from floor level to floor level is 15 feet in the basement and 12 feet for the ground and first floors. The average height of the loft is 4 feet.

4. The weight of the ceiling/floor for basement/ground floor and ground floor/first floor, consisting of plaster and joists with floor boards in each case is 20 pounds per square foot; the weight of the first floor ceiling plus roof joists and slates is 32 pounds per square foot.

5. A shielding building of similar size is 30 feet away from one of the long walls.

6. All windows are assumed to be solid wall and partition walls are regarded as being too thin to be significant.

The following is the calculation of the Protective Factor for the basement, ground and first floor rooms.

A. Basement

a. *Roof contribution.* The area is 30×60 sq ft and the height is 43 ft. The weight of the overhead material is 72 psf. From Table 17 at $\dfrac{\sqrt{1800}}{43-3} = 1.06$ and 72 psf we obtain a roof contribution of approximately 1.09 per cent.

b. *Wall contributions.* The square root of the area is 42.5 as obtained above and the weight of the wall material is 90 psf. From Table 20 with these values we obtain uncorrected wall contributions of 0.45 per cent for each wall.

i. Length correction factor for each shorter wall is $\dfrac{4 \times 30}{180} = 0.67$.

Length correction factor for each longer wall is $\dfrac{4 \times 60}{180} = 1.33$.

ii. Shielding correction factor for one longer wall for 30 feet distance is 0.5.

iii. Depth of basement correction factors for all four walls for 15 feet basement depth and area of 1800 square feet from Table 21 is 0.7 for each wall.

iv. Weight of ceiling correction factor for each wall contribution, using a figure of 20 psf basement ceiling weight is 0.25 (Table 22).

The total contributions then can be computed as follows:

Roof contribution $= 1.090\%$

Two shorter walls contributions: $2 \times 0.45 \times 0.67$
$\times 0.7 \times 0.25$ $= 0.105\%$

Unshielded longer wall contribution: 0.45×1.33
$\times 0.7 \times 0.25$ $= 0.105\%$

Shielded longer wall contribution: $0.45 \times 0.5 \times 1.33$
$\times 0.7 \times 0.25$ $= 0.053\%$

Total contributions $=$ say, 1.35%

Protective factor for basement room is $\dfrac{100}{1.35} = \underline{74}$

B. Ground Floor

a. *Roof contribution.* The area is 30 ft $\times$ 60 ft and the height is 28 ft. The weight of overhead material is 52 psf. From Table 17 at $\dfrac{42.5}{28-3} = 1.7$ we obtain a figure of 3.1 per cent for the roof contribution.

b. *Wall contributions.* Using a figure of 42.5 for the square root of the area and 90 psf for the weight of the walls, from Table 18 we obtain a figure of 2.0 for the uncorrected contribution through each wall.

The correction factors for length of walls and for shielding are the same as those obtained for the basement. These are 0.67 and 1.33 for the length of walls and 0.5 for shielding.

We can thus compute the total contributions as follows:

Roof contribution	$= 3.1\%$
Two shorter walls contribution: $2 \times 2.0 \times 0.67$	$= 2.7\%$
Unshielded longer wall contribution: 2.0×1.33	$= 2.7\%$
Shielded longer wall contribution: $2.0 \times 1.33 \times 0.5$	$= 1.3\%$
Total contributions	$= 9.8\%$

Protective factor $= \dfrac{100}{9.8} = \underline{10.1}$

C. First Floor

a. *Roof contribution*. Using A $= 1800$ and a height of 16 feet and overhead weight of 32 psf we obtain from Table 17 a roof contribution of 9.0 per cent.

b. *Wall contributions*. Using the data for the ground floor calculations and multiplying by the correction factor of 0.75 for a height of 12 feet above ground obtained from Table 19 we have the following computation:

Roof contribution	$= 9.0\%$
Two shorter walls contribution: $2 \times 2.0 \times 0.67 \times 0.75$	$= 2.0\%$
Unshielded longer wall contribution: $2.0 \times 1.33 \times 0.75$	$= 2.0\%$
Shielded longer wall contribution: $2.0 \times 1.33 \times 0.75 \times 0.5$	$= 1.0\%$
Total contributions	$= 14.0\%$

Protective factor $= \dfrac{100}{14.00} = \underline{7.1}$

Remembering the assumptions made at the beginning of this paragraph, the Protective Factors for a typical house structure may be summarised, as follows:

A Basement PF $= 74$
B Ground Floor PF $= 10$
C First Floor PF $= 7$

If the basement were only half below ground level, the PF would be roughly $\dfrac{74+10}{2} = 42.$

Table 17   Roof Contributions. Percentages of gamma radiation penetrating through the roofs of buildings of various dimensions

Height of overhead material in pounds per square feet of floor area	Percentage of radiation penetrating roof for values of $\sqrt{A}/(H-3)$, where A = the area of the roof and H = height from floor to average roof level, all in feet									
	0.5	1	1.5	2	3	4	5	6	7	8
0	0.75	2.3	4.8	7.4	12	16	20	23	24	26
20	0.6	1.8	3.8	5.8	9.8	13	15	17	18	19
40	0.45	1.4	3.0	4.7	7.3	9.0	9.8	10	10.2	10.5
60	0.36	1.1	2.1	3.1	4.3	5.2	5.4	5.6	5.7	5.8
80	0.28	0.85	1.6	2.2	2.8	3.0	3.1	3.1	3.2	3.3
100	0.21	0.6	1.1	1.5	1.8	1.9	1.9	1.95	1.95	2.0
120	0.14	0.14	0.7	0.9	1.05	1.1	1.1	1.15	1.15	1.15
140	0.1	0.27	0.45	0.56	0.65	0.69	0.69	0.69	0.70	0.70
160	0.064	0.18	0.30	0.37	0.41	0.43	0.43	0.43	0.44	0.44
180	0.044	0.12	0.19	0.24	0.28	0.30	0.30	0.30	0.30	0.30
200	0.030	0.08	0.13	0.16	0.18	0.18	0.18	0.18	0.18	0.18

Table 18   Wall Contributions. Percentages of gamma radiation penetrating through each wall of buildings to areas above the ground.

Weight of wall material in pounds per square foot	Percentage of radiation penetrating the wall for values of $\sqrt{A}$ the square root of the area in square feet									
	10	20	30	40	50	60	70	80	90	100
0	20	17	15	13	11.5	10.5	9.6	9.0	8.5	8.0
20	15	12	10	8.8	7.9	7.0	6.4	5.8	5.3	4.8
40	9.8	8.0	6.7	5.7	4.9	4.4	4.0	3.6	3.4	3.1
60	6.2	5.1	4.3	3.6	3.1	2.7	2.4	2.2	2.0	1.85
80	4.1	3.2	2.7	2.3	2.0	1.8	1.6	1.4	1.3	1.2
100	2.7	2.2	1.8	1.5	1.3	1.15	0.99	0.88	0.78	0.71
120	1.7	1.4	1.15	0.97	0.82	0.72	0.64	0.56	0.50	0.45
140	1.1	0.92	0.77	0.65	0.57	0.49	0.44	0.37	0.34	0.30
160	0.75	0.61	0.50	0.42	0.36	0.32	0.28	0.24	0.21	0.19
180	0.48	0.40	0.33	0.27	0.23	0.20	0.18	0.16	0.14	0.13
200	0.32	0.25	0.21	0.17	0.15	0.13	0.11	0.10	0.09	0.08

Table 19   Wall contribution correction factor for height above ground

Height of floor of room above ground in feet	Correction factor
4	1
17	0.7
30	0.6
50	0.5
86	0.4
144	0.3
260	0.2

Table 20   Basements. Penetration of gamma radiation through a wall to areas below ground

Weight of wall material in pounds per sq foot	Percentage of radiation penetrating wall to basement for values of $\sqrt{A}$									
	10	20	30	40	50	60	70	80	90	100
0–20	0.56	0.90	1.2	1.4	1.5	1.5	1.5	1.45	1.4	1.35
40	0.43	0.69	0.90	1.05	1.10	1.15	1.15	1.10	1.05	1.00
60	0.29	0.48	0.62	0.74	0.80	0.82	0.82	0.78	0.76	0.72
80	0.19	0.31	0.42	0.50	0.56	0.58	0.58	0.55	0.54	0.52
100	0.13	0.22	0.30	0.35	0.39	0.40	0.40	0.38	0.36	0.35
120	0.082	0.14	0.20	0.23	0.24	0.25	0.25	0.24	0.23	0.22
140	0.056	0.096	0.13	0.15	0.16	0.16	0.16	0.15	0.15	0.14
160	0.037	0.060	0.082	0.10	0.105	0.105	0.105	0.10	0.098	0.094
180	0.023	0.042	0.053	0.068	0.074	0.074	0.074	0.068	0.066	0.064
200	0.016	0.026	0.037	0.045	0.048	0.048	0.048	0.045	0.043	0.042

Table 21   Correction factor for depth of Basement

Area in sq ft	Depth of Basement in feet			
	15	20	30	40
100	0.4	0.2	0.05	0.01
500	0.6	0.3	0.1	0.05
2,500	0.8	0.6	0.4	0.2
10,000	0.8	0.7	0.6	0.4

Table 22   Correction factor for attenuation by Basement ceiling of scattered contributions from ground through walls and ceiling to basement

Weight of ceiling in pounds per sq ft	Correction factor
0	1
4	0.7
6	0.6
8	0.5
12	0.4
16	0.3
24	0.2
38	0.1
52	0.05
90	0.01
110	0.005
150	0.001

Survey of dwelling houses in the United Kingdom

9.19 Surveys have been made of different types of dwelling houses in the United Kingdom and their protective factors have been calculated for ground floor rooms in which it is assumed that there is no external door and the windows are solid walls. For this purpose it was assumed that the fallout is uniformly distributed and retained on the roof and on the ground around the building. The protective factors are shown in Table 23. The wide range in three or more storey buildings is due to variations in size, height and density of construction.

Table 23 Approximate protective factors in ground floor refuge rooms of typical British housing with timber upper floors and with windows and external doors blocked

Types of housing	Protective factor
Bungalow	5–10
Detached two-storey	15
Semi-detached two-storey 11 inch cavity walls	25–30
Semi-detached two-storey 13½ inch brick walls	40
Terraced two-storey	45
Terraced back-to-back	60
Blocks of flats and offices (see paragraph 9.1) Lower floors	50–500
second floor and above (decreasing)	50–20

9.20 The amount of fallout retained in the United Kingdom on a clean dry roof with a slope of about 30° (about 1 in 2) or more would be insignificant. If the roof were damp, most of the fallout would be retained until it becomes dry. Rainfall, other than a very light drizzle, would wash fallout off the roof. Consequently the protective factors of prepared refuges in most British houses may be higher than the values given in Table 23. Except in prolonged damp weather, the additional protection could be significant in houses with clean steep roofs having a low protective factor where a large part of the radiation is assumed to come from the roof.

Basements and trenches

9.21 A substantial increase in protection is obtained in cellars or basements, or in trenches under the floor. For example a trench under a detached two-storied house could give a PF of about 100 and a basement of between 50 and 100, if all the floor was 5 feet below ground level.

9.22 A properly constructed slit trench in the open with 3 feet of earth cover would have a protective factor of 200 or more.

Protection afforded by vehicles

9.23 The protective factors of various types of road transport are very low compared with buildings and would be about 1.5 or slightly more depending upon the size and weight of the vehicle, the height of the seating above ground and on the number of passengers. In passenger trains the protective factor would be equally low, between 3 and 5 depending upon the amount of fallout retained on the coach roof. In ships and boats away from land, protection would be significantly greater owing to the sinking of particles of fallout in water.

10 Hazards to Food, Water, Crops and Livestock

Entry of fission products into the human body

10.1 Over and above the main contact hazard described in paragraph 8.6 *et seq*, additional hazards to humans might arise from the consumption of:

a. products derived from animals grazing contaminated pastures or from fish caught in contaminated waters;

b. growing crops superficially contaminated by fallout;

c. superficially contaminated stored food or food in transit; and

d. contaminated water.

The extent of the consumption hazard would be governed by the level of radioactive fallout in the area from which the water and food are derived, the particle sizes, the degree of solubility of individual radioactive nuclides and the extent of accumulation in specific parts of plants or in particular animal organs. A large proportion of the ingested activity would pass through the gastro-intestinal tract and be excreted. Because of the longer residence time and concentration of material in the lower large intestine, this organ would tend to be the most heavily irradiated. The evidence suggests that doses of about 50r/day would be unlikely to produce any short term effects on this organ. Assuming simple precautions are taken over food, this dose-rate is not likely to be exceeded and the consequences of consuming contaminated food and water are markedly less than the consequences of environmental gamma radiation.

10.2 Radioactive iodine isotopes may be absorbed through the intestinal wall into the blood stream, and from one third to one half could reach and damage the thyroid gland before being excreted. Since milk constitutes the principal source of radioactive iodine, children would be at a higher risk of thyroid injury than adults in the immediate post-attack period. The risk would be virtually eliminated by the use of dried milk or milk substitutes (see paragraph 10.20 below).

10.3 A longer term ingestion hazard might arise from radioactivity taken into the plant through the roots and from the superficial contamination resulting from world wide fallout. The particle sizes and their solubility enhance the potential ingestion hazard in terms of radioactivity deposited per unit area, but at the same time only the longer lived nuclides would remain. This hazard should be discounted for home defence planning purposes.

Effect of fallout on sources of drinking water

10.4 It must be emphasized that gamma radiation does not in any way affect the purity or impair the potability of water. The main sources of drinking water in the United Kingdom are reservoirs fed from catchment areas, rivers and underground wells. Underground sources of water would be largely free from contamination but water stored in open reservoirs may be contaminated. In reservoirs and rivers many of the fallout particles would sink to the bottom or be held in mud or vegetation. There would be rapid reduction in radioactive concentrations, due to decay (see paragraphs 3.3 to 3.5) in the first two weeks after attack; thereafter, the rate of decrease would be comparatively slow, with reservoir supplies remaining contaminated longer than river water. If the source of supply could be satisfactorily monitored, then use of that source might be prevented for a time. Dangerous contamination of a source of supply would, however, have involved gamma radiation in the vicinity of the source at a level extremely hazardous to any person endeavouring to monitor that source, even if a satisfactory instrument could be developed for the purpose.

10.5 Supplies of drinking water are vital to human survival and to the survival of livestock. All sources of supply, whether contaminated or not, would need to be conserved. Since the hazard from environmental gamma radiation is much more significant than the hazard from contaminated water, the availability of minimal supplies within buildings during the initial period, and their sparing use, when people are taking cover in those buildings, would be of paramount importance.

Sewage disposal

10.6 The normal disposal of sewage depends at some stage on the action of micro-organisms and on an adequate supply of water. The risk of injury to the micro-organisms by fallout is neglible. The threat to water supplies has already been mentioned in paragraphs 10.4 and 10.5. In the event of widespread fallout in built-up areas, much of the fallout could be washed into street drains. Most of it would be trapped there until it decayed and it would not constitute a significant hazard because of the depth underground. Arrangements might be necessary to dispose of heavily contaminated drainage with the least harm to water supplies and sewage disposal.

Hazards to food stocks

10.7 After a nuclear attack, all sources of food will be of vital importance. Considerations which apply to processed and stored foods differ from those which apply to growing crops and livestock. Processed and stored foods in peacetime tend to be concentrated in industrial areas for ease of distribution. As part of the transition-to-war arrangements, considerable dispersal of stocks may be possible. In areas where nuclear bombs fall, stocks would be subjected to heat and blast effects. In all areas, stocks may be subject to contamination by fallout. On the other hand, the main hazard to crops and livestock would be from both the beta radiation arising from close contact with fallout particles and the environmental gamma radiation.

Processed and stored foods

10.8 Many factors have to be considered in assessing the damage to stored and processed foods by fallout. These include:

a. the extent of heat and blast damage to various types of building; and

b. the effects of fallout on different kinds of packaging.

Blast and heat damage

10.9 In terms of resistance to heat and blast, the weakest part of most modern food stores, which are often of single-storey light construction, is the roof which will easily lift and shatter to give an immediate missile hazard. The resistance to heat of this type of building is good because of the lack of inflammable and combustible materials on the exterior faces. Older multi-storied buildings are more prone to thermal damage but are more resistant to blast. The single-storey design exposes all the contents within to fallout if the roof is destroyed. The removal of the roof of a multi-storey building would expose only the contents of the top floor to fallout, although the contents on lower floors could become contaminated to a lesser extent by fallout entering through the damaged windows.

10.10 The primary blast wave forms missiles of broken glass, wood and roof splinters, as well as physically displacing food stacks and containers. This displacement, with its attendant breakages, is likely to cause the greatest damage. Missiles cause appreciable damage to food containers and may pose an additional problem of the removal of fragments before the food could be used. The primary blast wave is of less significance to the foods themselves, its main effect being the rupturing of pressure seals and shattering of some glass containers.

Fallout on foodstuffs

10.11 For health reasons food is usually surrounded by some form of packaging material or stored in some form of sealed container. Although some contamination would occur inside damaged containers (particularly those of paper, cardboard or sacking), the protection afforded by the building and the containers themselves would normally be sufficient to reduce the amount of fallout coming into contact with the stored food to such a low level that consumption of contaminated food would not result in a radiation dose to the gut in excess of 50r in one day. In the case of the ground floor of the building, 70 per cent of the fallout would probably be deposited within ten to fifteen feet of the ingress points: for large food stores with intact roofs, most of the food would not be materially affected by fallout contamination. With extensive roof damage, contamination would be more widespread. Because of its wetting effect and consequent penetration, fallout in droplet form would present a greater hazard than fallout of dry particles and it would be more difficult to remove.

10.12 Except in the case of coarse sacking, undamaged packages offer complete protection against dry fallout. For wet fallout however, only impervious materials, such as tins, glass jars and plastic bottles would obviate contamination. Cardboard boxes, fibre and paper sacks and bags are particularly vulnerable to wet contamination.

10.13 The major risk to perishable foods, such as meat and fish in cold stores comes not so much from the fallout as from the disruption of electricity supply. Food would be edible for only a short time before spoilation occurred, unless some other process of preservation could be quickly substituted. Other perishable foods such as vegetables and fruit are usually washed and perhaps peeled before consumption and these processes would substantially reduce the contamination hazard. Butter, margarine and cooking fats are normally separately wrapped and box-stored. Even if some box damage is sustained, these wrappings would usually be sufficient to prevent contamination of most of the contents.

10.14 Certain foods such as cereals, flour, sugar and vegetable oils are usually stored in bulk containers such as silos, before processing or packing. Silos, by virtue of their construction and shape, are resistant to blast damage. The most vulnerable part is the roof although, if it is removed contamination would occur only at the exposed surface of the stored food. Similarly, contamination of exposed mounds of foodstuffs would occur only as a surface phenomenon. Potatoes and root vegetables stored outside in clamps would be protected and safe to use. Hay or straw stacked before fallout and covered by tarpaulins would also be safe. Thus the removal of the top layer of the contaminated food would significantly reduce the risk.

10.15 Fallout is not a relevant factor for food actually in the process of manufacture. Blast damage to the factory itself and the disruption of power supplies would be the operative factors.

Fallout on crops

10.16 Radioactive fallout will contaminate large areas of crops and pasture. Direct contamination is a short term problem, being at a maximum immediately after the fallout deposition and decreasing with time as the radioactivity decays and the particles are removed by wind and rain. If the crops were consumed without an attempt to remove the adhering fallout particles, there could be an ingestion hazard. The usual methods of food processing and preparation would eliminate most of the risk, as is shown by the following examples:

Cereals—Wheat, barley etc. Fallout particles lodge mainly in the outer part of the ear. The threshing process and rejection of the husk fraction after milling would remove up to 90 per cent of the original contamination.

Root crops—Potatoes, beet etc. The direct contamination hazard to the root is negligible. Rejection of the contaminated tops, washing and/or peeling of the root would give almost complete decontamination.

Surface crops, open leaf—Cabbage, lettuce etc. The rough leaf and open structure of this class of vegetables could result in high retention of fallout particles. These vegetables, which have a low energy value, could be used after rejecting the outer leaves and washing the remainder.

Surface crops, legumes—Peas, beans etc. The pod structure of this class of vegetables provides a natural protective cover, and pod removal ensures almost complete decontamination.

Hard fruits—Apples, pears etc. The acts of washing and peeling provide almost 100 per cent decontamination.

Soft fruits—Plums, blackberries etc. This relatively minor source of food would be difficult to decontaminate.

Greenhouse vegetables—Tomatoes, lettuce etc. Contamination also occurs if the greenhouses are damaged. If the food inside is salvageable, washing in the the case of tomatoes and outer leaf removal and washing of the lettuce ensure adequate decontamination.

Losses of growing crops

10.17 Growing crops would be affected by the environmental gamma radiation from fallout particles on and around the crops (see paragraph 8.9). The fallout particles also emit beta radiation with an effective range of several feet in air and of a few centimetres in body or plant tissue (see paragraph 8.5). The damaging effects of fallout on growing crops would vary with different types of crop, the season and the stage in the growth cycle of each type of plant. When shoots are emerging and flower buds developing, these parts of the plant are vulnerable to radiation, particularly to contact beta radiation. Reasonable assessments of the likely overall losses on the harvest following a nuclear attack cannot yet be made. Further research is needed. The early post-strike intensity of fallout could also prevent or delay harvesting operations with consequent crop losses. The sowing and planting of essential crops could be similarly delayed.

Effect of fallout on livestock

10.18 Fallout particles could be retained on the coats of grazing animals: they could also be inhaled from or ingested with pasture. The animals would then suffer from the combined effects of external and internal beta radiation as well as those of environmental gamma radiation. In the case of cattle and sheep, fallout particles could be trapped and accumulate in the rumen with resultant ulceration and starvation. As far as possible, grazing animals would need to be brought under cover from fallout and given uncontaminated fodder and water. In affording protection, priority could be given to breeding stocks. Where cover is not available, the grazing area could be kept as small as possible. Because few isotopes accumulate in the flesh, animals that become sick from exposure to radiation, if slaughtered before death occurs from radiation sickness, would provide good clean meat. Care would need to be taken in removing the hide and offal.

Eggs, milk and fish

10.19 Eggs, derived from exposed but surviving animals, would not contain enough radioactivity to present a serious ingestion hazard. Most fission products are eliminated via the egg shells. Free-range hens would obviously be at greater risk of dying than those kept under cover. Thyroid damage from the consumption of eggs from apparently healthy poultry can be discounted.

10.20 The main ingestion hazard in the immediate post-attack period is presented by the consumption of milk and milk products, obtained from dairy cattle which have grazed contaminated pastures. Owing to the concentration of radioactive iodine in the animal thyroid and its rapid transfer into the milk, the radioiodine level would reach a maximum after about two to three days. The risk to children would be avoided by the use for, say, three weeks of milk powder, milk substitutes or milk from cows kept under cover and fed on uncontaminated fodder. Contaminated milk could be used to prepare products such as cheese or butter, where normal storage prior to consumption would allow the decay of the short-life iodine isotopes (see paragraph 10.2).

10.21 Radiation effects on freshly caught fish in the immediate post-attack period can be discounted. Shellfish and crustaceans from coastal areas of heavy fallout would constitute a risk but this source of food is relatively small.

Appendix I Atoms and the Structure of Matter: Some Definitions

1. A little knowledge of the structure of matter helps towards an understanding of the effects of nuclear weapons. Matter consists of an assembly of atoms of various ELEMENTS interspersed in space at relatively great distances from one another. The metals iron and aluminium, the non-metal sulphur and the gases hydrogen, oxygen and nitrogen are among the more common of the 105 different elements now known and some of these elements like plutonium are man-made. Each element has characteristic chemical properties by which it can be distinguished from all the other elements.

2. An ATOM of an element is the smallest particle which can exhibit the chemical properties of that element. For example, if single atoms of iron were broken up, the pieces would have the recognisable properties of quite different elements. Atoms are exceedingly small, far smaller than the limit of visibility under a microscope: nevertheless, most of the matter contained in each atom is concentrated in a central nucleus which is about 10,000 times smaller. A nucleus always carries one or more positive electrical charges and, in the normal state, it is surrounded by a cloud consisting of an equal number of negatively charged particles called ELECTRONS, so that the atom as a whole is electrically neutral. These electrons can be imagined as moving in orbits around the nucleus like planets around the sun.

3. A nucleus contains two main types of fundamental particle each of which is about 1,840 times as massive as the electron:

A NEUTRON with no electrical charge,
A PROTON with a positive charge.

Because of the repulsive forces between positive charges, nuclei cannot approach one another very closely, but an uncharged neutron can approach and hit another nucleus without being repelled. The energy released in an atomic reactor or in the detonation of a nuclear weapon is part of the large quantity of binding energy which holds the particles together in the nucleus.

4. The chemical properties peculiar to each element are determined by the number of protons, that is by the number of positive charges in the nucleus of each atom. Consequently, the elements can be numbered consecutively from the lightest element hydrogen (one proton with an electron in orbit around it) up to the largest atoms of the recently discovered element hahnium which have a nucleus containing 105 protons surrounded by a cloud of 105 electrons.

5. It is not possible for a nucleus to consist of protons alone, because the repulsive forces between the postive charges would make them fly apart: in nuclei containing more than one proton this is prevented by the presence of the neutrons and by the attractive forces between the different fundamental particles in close proximity. The atoms of all the elements, with the exception of the simplest type of hydrogen atom, contain at least as many neutrons as protons. The larger the nucleus, the greater is the excess of neutrons over protons needed to hold the nucleus together.

6. All atoms of one element contain the same number of protons but they may have different numbers of neutrons. Thus, several atomic species of the same element are possible and these are called ISOTOPES of that element. There is a limit to the number of possible isotopes of each element and those which contain too many or too few neutrons are unstable or radioactive and disintegrate sooner or later, by expelling neutrons or electrons (resulting from the conversion of neutrons to protons) in order to restore the balance in the ratio of neutrons to protons needed for stability. In those circumstances the electron expelled at high speed from the nucleus is called a beta particle. A succession of changes or disintegrations may occur before a stable nucleus is formed and, in many of these, excess energy may be emitted also in the form of gamma rays, an electromagnetic radiation like light or X-rays but of much shorter wavelength. A frequent occurrence, particularly among heavier radioactive atoms, is the expulsion of an alpha particle which is, in fact, the nucleus of the gaseous element helium (containing two protons and two neutrons) without its two outer electrons.

7. The element uranium found in nature is a mixture of isotopes but most of it consists of atoms with 92 protons and 146 neutrons, a total of 238 mass units in each nucleus: hence, this isotope is referred to as U-238. Another isotope, U-235, with 92 protons and 143 neutrons found in natural uranium to the extent of about 0.7 per cent was the explosive material used in the first atomic bomb after separation from the U-238.

8. The plutonium isotope Pu-239 (94 protons plus 145 neutrons) is an artificial one produced in an atomic reactor from U-238 and the isotope of uranium U-233 is produced similarly from thorium. All three of the above isotopes can be used as explosive charges in nuclear weapons.

9. Uranium and plutonium are heavy metals near the end of the consecutive list of elements. At the other end of the list, the lightest element hydrogen has two additional rarer isotopes and all three have nuclei containing only one proton. One of these is called deuterium because of its two units (one proton plus one neutron) and the other tritium because of its three units (one proton plus two neutrons). Both deuterium and tritium are used directly or indirectly as the nuclear explosive charge in a thermo-nuclear or hydrogen bomb.

Nuclear fission
10. The isotopes U-233, U-235 and Pu-239 are radioactive and their atoms disintegrate by expelling alpha or beta particles with gamma rays from the nuclei. But there is another way in which these atoms can break up; when they capture, or are hit by, a neutron each nucleus splits up into two not quite equal parts. At the same time, two or three other neutrons are released. This fission process is responsible for the large quantities of nuclear energy released in an atomic reactor or in the detonation of a nuclear weapon. The fissile charge even in a small nuclear weapon although it may weigh only several pounds, contains multiple millions of atoms and these do not all split up in quite the same way. The products of fission contain therefore about 200 different radioactive isotopes of about 35 elements.

Critical sizes of fissile charges
11. When a piece of fissile material is below a certain critical size, a few of the atoms are continually undergoing fission, but more neutrons escape from its surface than are produced in fission and prevent the build-up of an increasing chain of fissions. If several pieces of fissile material, totalling more than the critical amount, are suddenly brought together inside a strong container or tamper a nuclear detonation results. The critical size depends upon a number of factors including whether the material is solid metal or in a porous, spongy form, the nature of the container and whether it absorbs neutrons or can reflect them back into the fissile charge.

12. Published information suggests that an unconfined sphere of U-235 metal of about $6\frac{1}{2}$ in. diameter and weighing about 48 kilogrammes would be a critical amount: this would be reduced to about $4\frac{1}{2}$ in. diameter (16 kg) for a U-235 sphere enclosed in a heavy tamper. The critical sizes for U-233 and Pu-239 have not been disclosed but are somewhat smaller than for U-235. The increasing mechanical complication of bringing together, rapidly and simultaneously, a number of sub-critical pieces of fissile material sets a practical limit to the power of nuclear fission weapons.

Nuclear fission and thermo-nuclear weapons

13. A temperature of several million degrees centigrade is reached in the detonation of a nuclear fission weapon. At this temperature atoms are stripped of most of their surrounding cloud of electrons and the nuclei move at very high speeds experiencing many collisions with one another. In these circumstances the nuclei of the rarer hydrogen isotopes deuterium and tritium have enough energy of motion to overcome the repulsive forces between their single positive electrical charges and they are able to fuse together. The energy released in the fusion of these two nuclei is about one-twelfth of that released in the fission of a single U-235 nucleus, but on an equal weight basis, the fusion energy is about two and a half times as large as the energy of fission of U-235.

14. In the process of fusion a neutron is released at a very high speed from each pair of reacting nuclei and it has enough energy to cause fission of the atoms of U-238. Thus, if U-238 is used as the bomb case in a thermo-nuclear weapon the quantity of fission products will be increased many times (see paragraph 1.6). This type of weapon is the fission-fusion-fission type or so-called 'dirty' bomb.

15. Deuterium and tritium as isotopes of the gaseous element hydrogen have to be liquefied at a very low temperature and maintained there for containment in a thermo-nuclear weapon. This is inconvenient although it has been reported that the first American H-bomb tested in 1952 was of this type. In later weapons the deuterium is combined chemically with the metal lithium in the form of a white powder. Each neutron (1 mass unit) released by the triggering fission bomb splits a lithium atom (6 mass units) into the non-radioactive gas helium (4 mass units) and tritium (3 mass units) and the latter fuses with the deuterium atoms present in the compound. There is no limit, other than the convenience of delivery, to the size of a fusion or thermo-nuclear weapon. Lithium deuteride may be less costly than fissile materials such as U-233, U-235 or Pu-239.

16. Helium gas, the main product of a thermo-nuclear detonation, is NOT radioactive (hence the expression 'clean' bomb) but the very high speed neutrons which are also emitted collide with other atoms. They may collide with the nitrogen atoms in the atmosphere and release a very intense and penetrating form of gamma radiation (flash). They may induce intense radioactivity in some of the ground material if the weapon is burst on the ground—but this decays rapidly in a few days.

Appendix II   Scaling Laws

Shock waves

1. Blast damage from nuclear detonations depends primarily upon the peak pressure in the shock wave and the associated wind pressure but also to some extent on the duration of the shock wave. The peak pressure and wind pressure decrease rapidly with increasing distance from the explosion (see Table 24 below).

A comparison of the blast effects of two detonations W_1 and W_2 kilotons in power is best made at points of EQUAL PEAK SHOCK PRESSURE. The comparison can then be made of the distances D_1 and D_2 of these points from the respective explosions, of the times t_1 and t_2 taken for the shock waves to arrive at these points and of the lengths of time (durations) L_1 and L_2 of the positive pressure phase at these points. All are related to the cube root of the weapon yield thus:

i. $D_2 = D_1 \sqrt[3]{\dfrac{W_2}{W_1}}$

ii. $t_2 = t_1 \sqrt[3]{\dfrac{W_2}{W_1}}$

iii. $L_2 = L_1 \sqrt[3]{\dfrac{W_2}{W_1}}$

D_2 and D_1 must be in the same units, as must also be t_2 and t_1, as well as L_2 and L_1.

Example: For weapons $W_1 = 20$ KT and $W_2 = 10$ MT.

$$\sqrt[3]{\frac{W_2}{W_1}} = \sqrt[3]{500} = \text{approximately 8.}$$

Hence $D_2 = 8\ D_1$; $t_2 = 8\ t_1$ and $L_2 = 8\ L_1$

Table 24 Relation between static overpressure, wind pressure and wind velocity for detonations near sea level. (*Taken from the US publication* Effects of Nuclear Weapons (1964), *page 107*)

Peak static overpressure* (psi)	Peak wind pressure (psi)	Maximum blast wind speed (miles per hour)
72	80	1,170
50	40	940
30	16	670
20	8	470
10	2	290
5	0.7	160
2	0.1	70

* ie pressure above that of the atmosphere (14.7 psi). Reflected overpressures can be very much higher (paragraph 7.3)

Dimensions of the crater from a ground burst weapon

2. The dimensions of the crater (without the lip) from a 1 KT weapon burst on saturated clay are: diameter about 210 ft and depth about 18 ft. Scaling factors for various types of ground are given in Table 25 for a bomb of W KT yield. The diameter scales as the cube root and the depth as the fourth root of the weapon power.

Table 25   Crater scaling factors

Nature of the Ground	Dimensions of crater without the lip	
	Radius (feet)	Depth (feet)
Saturated clay	105 ⎤	18 ⎤
Dry soil	63 $\left.\right\} \sqrt[3]{W}$	25 $\left.\right\} \sqrt[4]{W}$
Hard Rock	53 ⎦	20 ⎦

NOTE: The radius of the crater with its lip is roughly twice that of the crater alone

Volume of crater $= \pi \times (\text{radius})^2 \times \dfrac{(\text{depth})}{2}$

Fireball dimensions

3. Maximum diameter $= 460W^{0.4}$ (in feet for W in KT). There is no simple scaling law for thermal effects of weapons of different powers (see paragraphs 5.5 and 5.9).

Stabilised cloud: heights and dimensions

4. The location of a nuclear detonation would normally be determined by instruments (see paragraph 3.6). If not, it might be possible to estimate these approximately from observations of the stabilised cloud, about 10 minutes after the detonation, when the cloud has ceased to rise but its form has not yet been significantly affected by the high altitude winds. Such observations would be the azimuthal bearings of the stem from which the burst could be located by

triangulation, the angles of elevation from the observers to the cloud top or base or the bearing angles of the cloud diameter.

As indicated in paragraph 8.20, when the yield of a nuclear weapon is less than 100 KT, the cloud tends to become spherical in shape, while clouds from weapons of 100 KT or greater, appear as flat cylindrical discs on top of a cylindrical stem that is roughly one tenth the diameter of the cloud disc. From these observations and using the data in Table 26, the location and yield of a nuclear weapon detonation could be estimated roughly in the absence of sophisticated instruments and methods.

Table 26   Cloud heights and diameters

Yield	Cloud top height 10^3 feet	Cloud base height 10^3 feet	Cloud diameter miles
20 MT	123	73	76
10 MT	107	63	58
5 MT	94	57	44
2 MT	80	49	30
1 MT	71	45	24
0.5 MT	63	39	17
100 KT	47	31	8
20 KT	35	23	4.5

Contour areas

5. When scaling from 100 per cent fission yield to any other fission yield, the *areas* of the fallout contours remain the same but the dose-rates scale in direct proportion to the fission yield.

Time taken by particles of different sizes to fall from different altitudes

6. Fallout within the limits of the downwind dose-rate contours is expected to consist mainly of radioactive particles within the size range of 350 to 75 microns and the descent times are set out in Table 27. For a 10 MT weapon the activity in the cloud will be almost entirely below 80,000 ft.

Table 27   Time in hours for rough particles of different sizes to fall to the ground from specific heights

Particle size microns:	500	350	200	100	75
Falling to ground from	hours	hours	hours	hours	hours
80,000 ft	1.6	2.3	4.5	12	22
60,000 ft	1.3	2.0	3.7	9.5	17
40,000 ft	1.0	1.5	2.8	6.8	12
30,000 ft	0.8	1.2	2.2	5.3	9

Conversion data

7. Table 28 contains information for conversion to and from international (SI) units.

Table 28   Conversion of relevant British and non-SI units to equivalent values in SI units

1 micron (micrometre)	{ one thousandth of 1 millimetre { one millionth of 1 metre
1 inch	25.4 millimetres
1 foot	0.305 metres
1 mile	1.609 kilometres
1 square foot	0.093 square metres
1 square mile	2.59 square kilometres
1 foot per second	0.3049 metres/sec
1 mile/h (mph)	1.609 kilometres/h
1 gallon	4.546 dm³
1 lb force (0.4536 kg force)	4.448 newtons
1 lb per square inch (1 psi)	6895 newtons/sq metre
1 psf	47.9 newtons/sq metre
1 calorie (Btu=252 cal.)	4.187 joules
1 KWH (1 HPH=0.746 KWH)	3.6×10^6 joules
1 Watt	{ 1J/sec { 1NM/sec
1 dyne	10^{-5} newtons

Centigrade—The metric practical unit of temperature is the degree Celsius (°C).

Printed in England for Her Majesty's Stationery Office by
Brightman & Stratton Ltd.
Dd 716552 K40 12/80